MW00984076

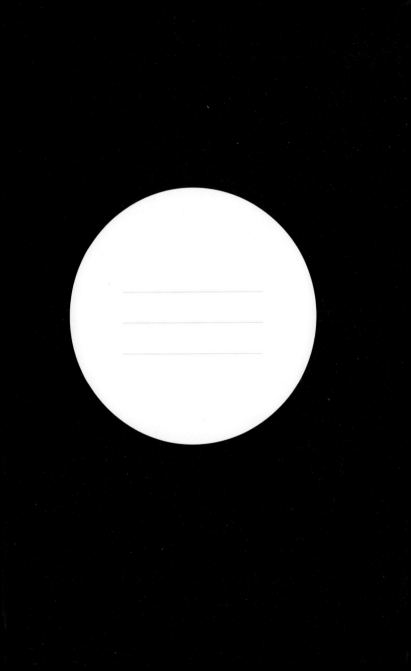

LOSS

'The honesty, wisdom and pain of this writing add up to something very important: truth. Siddharth Dhanvant Shanghvi writes with unflinching truth about the unbearable, and thus makes it, at least, comprehensible'
– SALMAN RUSHDIE, author of *Midnight's Children*

'A remarkable meditation on grief, legacy, and the pathways out of anguish'
– DAVID EBERSHOFF, author of *The Danish Girl*

'*Loss* is a finely tuned reflection on the death of parents, the effects of orphaning, a sustained search in which you'll hear echoes of your own relationship with death and parents because at each moment Shanghvi opens outward toward vision instead of remaining mired in sorrow. You'll be delighted by the flexibility and turns of an elegant mind'
– DAVID VANN, author of *Legend of a Suicide*

SIDDHARTH DHANVANT SHANGHVI

'Siddharth Dhanvant Shanghvi's literary forebears are
Somerset Maugham, Graham Greene, and E.M. Forster.
He's also an original, a major storyteller who beguiles us into
a world of illusion and bestows us with a sharp-eyed lens
into the heart'
– AMY TAN, author of *The Joy Luck Club*

'One of the most talented young Indian novelists'
– ARAVIND ADIGA, author of *The White Tiger*

'Dazzling'
– JOHN BERENDT, author of
Midnight in the Garden of Good and Evil

THE HOUSE NEXT DOOR: PHOTOGRAPHS

'There is a beautiful sense of a charged melancholy in these images. You can sense the calm in how the house is arranged and appreciate the simple compositions, as if life has stalled as we wait for the Father to respond, and for life to move slowly forward'
– MARTIN PARR, photographer, *Only Human*

'Siddharth has used the camera to enhance a parallel world to his poetic words. When the two media are combined, word and images, a deep and unforgettable vision is realized'
– ROGER BALLEN, photographer,
Ballenesque – Roger Ballen: A Retrospective

LOSS

Essays

SIDDHARTH

DHANVANT

SHANGHVI

HarperCollins*Publishers*India

First published in hardback in India in 2020 by
HarperCollins *Publishers* India
A-75, Sector 57, Noida, Uttar Pradesh 201301, India
www.harpercollins.co.in

2 4 6 8 10 9 7 5 3 1

P-ISBN: 978-93-5357-598-4
E-ISBN: 978-93-5357-599-1

Book design by Bonita Vaz-Shimray
Typeset in 11/14 Garamond Premier Pro

Printed and bound at Thomson Press (India) Ltd
🅕🅘🅞🅞🅞HarperCollinsIn

'We were together. I forget the rest'
– Walt Whitman

For Parul & Nehal

Contents

Introduction

Between 2008 and 2018 I lost my father, my mother, and my dog. This was sad but not tragic – people do lose their parents and their pets; this is a rite of passage, an inescapable fact, an initiation into adulthood, an ascension from the fear of death to a recognition of its inevitable event. But no one is okay with dying: perhaps because life has been anything but okay, all the remarkable bits fade, and at the end we come to count our greatest wins as insights into ourselves, and into the awful things that happened to us, if only to set them aside. It is a little like organizing your drawer of socks; you match them, you roll one into the other, carefully, affectionately, and then when the tedious task is done you think – I did all this for a drawer of

socks? Of course, life makes abundant room for joy, for pleasure;
I certainly found tremendous pleasure in the three lives that
make up this book – their laughter, their conversation, their
presence is their best thing, and still lives on, ahead of death.

Maybe that's all there is to it: language, how we employ it to
know someone, or love them more deeply.

—

This book was to come out in the spring of 2020. But then, the
pandemic had broken. The deaths I had encountered – of the
ones I loved – grew into a life lesson, a scholarship of the times, a
primer for one. This is how you die. This is what you must leave
behind: everything. These are the people to thank. Pay your
bills. Even if it's a sock drawer, leave it pretty, or at the very least:
neat. What matters is how you make someone feel. This book
was an organization of socks inside socks, which is to say it was
an ordinary thing that had to be done. Meanwhile, death was
an extraordinary thing staring at us through the window of a
terrible, terrible year. Like a mirror devouring a mirror, the events
of my parents' deaths swallowed me so I could write this book, a
reflection over life's opposite thing, its redemption, its truth, its
purpose, its meaning. My parents had been teaching me how to
leave the room after the party. A friend said she imagined that I
wore only black at home, which couldn't be farther from the truth.

—

Every day in Goa, wild birds animate my garden. Hornbills emit a strange, hollow honking, their wingspans formidable when in flight. Baya weavers cry out in a ceremonious pomp, excitedly, in a heat of birdly gossip. The mechanical rattle of a kingfisher, a flash of winged blue piercing through rice fields. Sometimes when their sounds overlap, and intersect, an orchestra of shrieks and melodic repeats and a gap forms into which the sorrows run through.

The best answers are the ones we fall into, like love.

Briefly, this evening, I felt as if I had come very far, and only just begun. Yonder, western sky, orange with traces of aluminium. Peacocks roost in the mango tree while evening bleeds light out of the horizon. But in a few hours, it will be a new day, another one, imagine – the thrill, promise, delight, the endless possibilities of another day.

——

Dhanvant'

It's the phone call you dread – yet fully expect.

'Papa passed away,' my sister said through muffled sobs. 'He died,' she repeated, as if I might not have understood her the first time around.

I was in Jaisalmer. It was February. My father had passed in his sleep in Bombay. My sister was in Bangalore.

Slowly collecting between these three cities was a silent pool of loss.

We would have to wade through it now and come over to the other side.

—

I had to drive from Jaisalmer to Jodhpur, where I would catch a flight to Bombay; the road journey takes four hours. The hotel manager came to see me off at daybreak. A waiter held the brown leather leashes of two golden retrievers, handsome and bouncing, the gold feathering on their forelegs fluttering in the January wind. The magnificent hotel looked like a fort that I was leaving behind, as if I was going away on battle. I had to be home in time to make sure the last rites would be performed. Placing efficiency before feeling, I alternated between phone calls, arranging flight and funeral details with clinical detachment.

I have never properly remembered the lines of Emily Dickinson:

Because I could not stop for Death –
He kindly stopped for me –
The Carriage held but just Ourselves –
And Immortality.

In the car, I tried to think, was it *And Immortality* or *Or Immortality*? Perhaps the driver, whose tanned, smooth face I caught in halves in the rear-view mirror thought me crazy – distraught, then trying to remember something, now speaking on the phone formally, solemnly, performing my grief because I had not yet fully met its force, and dismantling, speaking of my father's death with an uncle in a formal tone, as if delivering a valedictorian speech. During a lull in my phone calls, my driver pointed out the makeshift cow stations along the highway. 'There was an eclipse last night,' he said.

'It's auspicious to feed cattle.' Later, I would reflect on his kindness: how he, a stranger, led me to a timeless ritual either as a form of distraction or as kind of redemption rite. We stopped. I got out – the air was cold, the sun was clear, strong. Great big trucks loomed by. After buying thick bundles of grass from a shepherd, I threw them out to the spindly cows huddled on the slopes flanking the highway. Hurriedly, hungrily, they ate this offering. Behind the cows was dry brown undergrowth, and above, the canvas of a grave clear blue sky. Flocks of little black birds thinned out into the sky. I wondered if they were coming home, or if they were just leaving.

Considering death is like plunging your hands into a pond: encountering shapes you cannot name, facing alien textures, you know only that everything is slippery and dark – and that you are glad to be standing outside of it, on dry land. *As of yet*. I was on land now, staring at black birds in the great sky, while my father was being bathed and dressed by priests for fire. John Donne believed death was an ascension to a better library. Maybe what this implied was that death was freedom from language, a world where everything was already known, deciphered, felt, finally, as it were, without cues or subtext, an awareness or sentience without comparison. It was, perhaps, a kind of true seed knowledge – a key to the safe.

My father's last meal had been a big bowl of strawberries and fresh cream; he had liked it so much he had asked for a second portion. Then he had gone to bed and he never got up – he had suffered a heart attack. The death of a king, or just someone dreadfully lucky.

——

THE Hindu funereal ritual is called *antyesti*, which translates roughly into 'the final sacrifice'. The body is prepared at home. The corpse is washed, covered in a white cloth (a woman whose husband is still alive is sometimes covered in red cloth). At the cremation ground the body is placed on a pyre, the feet facing south. In some iterations of the ceremony, I had read, the lead cremator – either a priest or the eldest son – ends the service by poking the burning skull with a stave. Through the resultant hole, the spirit is believed to be finally relieved. It jumps out of the body, free of its form, and the weight of this form. I thought: that's *me*. I was going to have to do that to my father. When the terror of this fact abated, I thought it was a little like writing, words freed from the mind, from imagination, free at long last. I did not think this a good recommendation for writing: to compare it to skull stabbing, but perhaps it is a version of that.

–

When my sister had called me in Jaisalmer, sobbing, one of my first feelings – in addition to sadness and disbelief – was of cold relief. The last ten years of my father's life had cost him his independence, his mind, and the full dignity of presence. There had been painful rounds of chemo in a battle with lymphoma of the brain. The disease, and its equally toxic cure, ravaged his brain, leaving him with memory loss and cognitive dissonance while the rest of him – the physical him – was perfectly intact. So he looked fine, he had no physical handicap, but his mind – his cognition, his memory, his aptitude for pleasure – was failing him, one day at a time. The doctor said this was not directly connected to his cancer but to his age, to an all-round attrition of time.

This decade had been a revelation for my father, but also for his children. 'There is a certain part of all of us that lives outside of time,' Kundera wrote. I saw this most clearly with my father, in the years leading up to his death. My father had entered the years of his life that would be lived outside of time. This is characterized by insipid hours that gnaw into you like a colony of white ants as you stand helpless before fate's determined indifference; without a strong mind, a vigorous imagination and an instinct for love, there is only erosion. This is all right until life makes you a witness of your own erosion, which is when you realize this a game where all the rules are wired against you, and even if you win, you will still die.

Many key western classical texts split life between the tragic and the comic mode. Aristophanes wrote some pretty bawdy plays with bad jokes. Stradella understood our appreciation of the farcical and shaped the genre of *opera buffa*. Sophocles and Aeschylus wrote tragedies that influenced Shakespeare and, latterly, Beckett. But perhaps the masters did not heed that life's essential mode was one of rapturous boredom: a long, dull run of nothing. My father's final decade was utterly monotonous for him; life on repeat mode – wake, bathe, eat, sleep, wake, eat, sleep – turned out deathlier than death itself.

In cruel counterpoint to my father's gentle, incremental effacement, my mother had lived out her final years in savage bursts of physical pain: defeated by arthritis, entirely bedbound in her final decade, suffering distinguished her end. She screamed from her hospital bed in the ICU – asking, begging, to be put out of this awful, unbearable shape her form had veered into, like a mythic creature from a minor but important tragedy. But in the case of my father, death had behaved itself, plucking existence out of him expertly, as if a set of divine tweezers had been used for a tidy, quick conclusion. The comparison of deaths – between that of my father and my mother – provoked impossible questions in my siblings and me. Why did our mother suffer so? Why was our father's end so peaceful? Who decides? The *Bardo Thodol*, the classic Tibetan text, is about preparing the soul for the state between rebirths, when one sheds one's physical form.

But I had come to see that preparation for death could start much sooner, when we are still a way from either illness or death.

——

A<small>T</small> my house in Goa hangs a photograph that I made of my father having his lunch. I shot him from the floor above him, looking down at him. This aerial shot shows my father at the head of a long, lonely table; the eight chairs descending down, on either side of the table, are unoccupied, utensils are scattered over the cream tablecloth. The thali would likely contain my father's favourite mug-ni-daal, rice, pickles, a rotla. The photograph, taken after my father was recovered from his cancer, radiates loneliness, grief, absence; its peculiar arresting isolation is like a monk's chamber, bare but with spiritual purpose. In the last nine years of his life, my father was widowed, his brain cancer had eaten into his ability for conversation (which he now performed on rote, asking us the same four obvious questions before resigning to an expansive, unsettling silence). Instead of facing the garden, my father sat looking at a wooden screen that divided the living room from the dining area – it would seem odd that he didn't want to look out at his beloved kadam trees, his border of palms, the small square spit of lawn. His back was to all the growing things. When my sisters and I saw his usual sense of fiery independence and self-sufficiency devolve into impenetrable desperation – old age is a clumsy articulation of life – we wondered if he was better off without this span of time after his cancer.

We are allowed to leave the room while we're still having fun.

—

In my father's case, this door first creaked open when he was seventy: he was diagnosed with cancer. He was not terribly old but youth was long behind him. Important events had been enjoyed, and more of his prayers, in balance, had been answered than not. His excellent doctor was right, I suppose, in telling him that he could beat cancer (which he did – and, extraordinarily, for his kind of cancer, and the age when he had it, he suffered no relapse). Dominant culture celebrates those who 'fight back' and 'overcome', while surrender and submission are too often mistaken for defeat. My father did beat his cancer – but what followed? Illness, loneliness and simple old age profoundly impaired his pleasure in living towards the end of his life. Staring into space is a terrible way to spend one's time because, well, there is no end to space. Would it have been better for him to allow his first brush with cancer, at an age when he had already witnessed and experienced most things that he had wished to see and know, to take him? My sisters and I think about this a lot, about him and also about what we might do, were we handed a similar diagnosis in our old age. In an essay for *Granta*, Murakami writes,

> There is one thing I can say for certain: the older a person gets, the lonelier he becomes. It's true for everyone. But maybe that isn't wrong. What I mean is, in a sense our lives are nothing more than a series of stages to help us get used to loneliness. That being the case, there's no reason to complain. And besides, who would we complain to anyway?

As a single person, I place particular emphasis on the idea of leaving the party with my shoes on; there's going to be no one to drive me home. John Irving cautions against living so long that it results in turning into a caricature of oneself. After watching my father's powerful loneliness billow and expand – a time in which all the things that had had once potent meaning were hollowed out – I told myself: leave, if you've enjoyed yourself. Leave, because you are still enjoying yourself. Leave, because you will have to anyway.

Learn to see when the right time is staring you in the face. *Leave*.

Our exit from this world is remembered far more than our entry into it.

—

There is a protocol for when someone dies. It is simple: *be present*.

People will forget if you came for a birthday party or a wedding but they will always hold it against you if you don't show up when someone they love has died. Our old neighbours, considered genteel Gujaratis with whom my father played badminton in Parle, who wolfed down my Baa's khandvi, who my mother speciously considered 'khandaani', never turned up. Neither did many friends, including a man my father dropped home every day after his work for years. A woman I worked with closely on art projects in Goa sent me a WhatsApp message expressing her condolence. For over seven years we had known each other, we had eaten at each other's homes at dinners, we had celebrated birthdays together, rejoiced over shows, shared confidences, exchanged ideas, insights and fears. Initially, I was hurt, then angry, and finally, her absence for my father's death eclipsed all her presence in my life; suddenly, permanently, she became a non-person, dead to me even while she was alive. A death exposes the living as they are. Elephants have been documented to return to the body of a deceased member of their group; dolphins have been recorded spending days with the carcass of one of their pod. It's as if they want to tell something that is no longer there that they are still there; or perhaps they consider, without sentimentality, without verifiable proof, that something like the soul still hovers around the decaying flesh, dazzled that it has shed the garb. Studies have shown chimpanzees express 'greater affiliation' to a mother who is mourning her dead young; giraffe mothers lay vigil over a dead calf for days before finally walking away from the corpse. Grief and separation distress have been documented in other animals as various as cows, goats and even chickens.

Not all of us need to learn from animals, but evidently some of us do.

—

Among the mourners was Gopal, who my father had helped

secure a job as a peon, over two decades ago. He showed up one afternoon, waited on the sofa, his face in his hands. The visit was unexpected. Hardly had I sat down when Gopal began to howl. I didn't know what to say to him. I was aware of the disparity – he was poor, I was rich; he was consoling me, I was inconsolable. I knew now what Iris Murdoch meant by 'bereavement is my occupation and it absorbs me completely'. In spite of our differences, Gopal and I had never been more equal, I felt, as I sat before an ordinary man who recalled how my father had 'changed his life' by doing something very simple: by giving him a job. He continued howling. I was embarrassed by this show until I realized I was equally embarrassed by my own grief. And I was also shocked when I felt, out of nothing, that I truly longed for everyone I had lost – lovers, friends – but I did not miss them at all.

In Gopal's grief ran traces of a gratitude that was greater than fondness, and something I could relate to. My father's accomplishments included founding a school (and keeping me out of jail until the age of eighteen). It was in this school that Gopal had landed a job. 'My kids are doing well. They are educated. They will find good jobs,' he said to me. 'It is all a blessing.' I looked at him, his glassy moist eyes, and thought: Yes, it is all a blessing, even this brief encounter, when you bared your sadness. It is a blessing you have a job. It is a blessing my father had the money for cancer treatment. It is a blessing that while such deaths can cleave you to the bone, I am still speaking with you as if nothing had ever happened and congratulating you on the success of your children. It is a blessing that you came, Gopal, thank you, *thank you with all my heart*.

When someone dies, show up. There's not much else to show. Text messages – even meaningful ones – cannot honour a life. The time for eloquence is replaced by presence. Facebook comments are digital dust – no one is interested in watching you perform grief with an emoticon.

Send khichdi. Bring lunch. Drop off a book. Check in on the ones you love.

And remember that you're being watched from a far up place.

So just put on a clean shirt and go.

–

I wish I could say that loss, and the grieving that accompanies it, makes you a better person. Mostly, I have found, loss exhausts you; often, it leaves you bitter. And yet it gifts the living something powerful: detachment, a cool cleanness, for seeing people as they are, so that you might love them without having to like them.

I'll give you an example: at my father's funeral we saw an older relative; my family had been estranged from him, after harsh words had been exchanged. Nevertheless, this old man with his large beaked nose – who had known my father intimately and for much longer than his children ever had – was hunched at the crematorium to pay him his respects; he was there to commit a last, filial fondness. There it was then, the great levelling hand of death, smoothening the creases from the past, reminding mortals how minor quarrels are nothing before its might. In that moment, my heart filled with something like forgiveness for my older relative's regrettable past conduct. I forgot my resentment for him simply because he was grieving for my father. This reminded me that while I did not appreciate his morals, and what he had done in lieu of them, I could clearly glimpse underneath his ribs a fine animal heart bleeding with sorrow. It was like an elephant visiting a deceased member of its kin, or a monkey gathering with other monkeys around a dead monkey. Human of heart, animal by instinct.

Or maybe my heart did not well up with forgiveness.

Perhaps it was just acceptance. My acceptance of this strange, stubborn man who in his nineties was rippling with sorrow for the death of my father. In the end, the only thing we can do for anyone, beyond loving them, is simply to acknowledge them as they are, for who they are, even if it is to let them go from our lives. ('Understanding is love's other name,' the Buddhist sage Thich Nhat Hanh says.)

A while later I reflected on why my grudge melted away so cleanly at the funeral. I had been overwhelmed by the feeling then that we were all simply in the holding pen of life, and that this is how we were all going to end up: dead, like my father. It did not matter, nothing did, certainly not my grudges. What we do in our lives differentiates us – some labour tirelessly, others enjoy martinis at lunch. We are single, married or widowed, dark or fair, trivial or smart. Yet the permutations of our uniqueness are no match for what unites us: love. Quoting a line from her husband the poet Nick Laird, Zadie Smith made a beautiful epigraph in one of her novels – 'time is how you spend your love'.

So, what is the opposite of this idea? All the time you do not spend with love is not time but its opposite, a kind of anti-fate, anti-time, the far corner of life, close to annihilation but without its attendant relief.

Give love. Receive love too. It is the only thing you take with you when you die, and because it is eternal, so are you.

——

AFTER my mother died, I sensed her disperse into formlessness: she was suddenly everywhere. Naturally, I was terrified. (Was she, from her heavenly perch, keeping tabs on my drinking habit?) I wanted her back in her body, or at least without this third-person perspective: the omnipresent Voice of Mother. But that wasn't going to ever happen. I dreamed about my father for days after he died. Once, I woke and sat up in my bed, soaked in tears. I'd been crying in my sleep, bewildered by my pain and amazed at when and how it occurred. 'Grief, when it comes, is nothing like we expect it to be,' Joan Didion wrote in her memoir, *The Year of Magical Thinking.* By this time, I'd begun to see myself not as a son but as an orphan: my parents were gone. The word orphan, at its Latinate root (which is cognate also with the Sanskrit), means to be *bereaved*. The etymology of the word bereaved leads us back to multiple meanings but the old Church Slavonic root means 'slave' or alternately 'rabota' – servitude. Are we enslaved to the memory of the person we have lost? Does a version of our self live under the skin of this memory? One of the smallest species of antelope, the dik-dik, marks its territory with tears. That is what memory is like – a marking of sacred turf – with the force of remembrance.

Some months after my father's death, I was at the Shreenath-ji Temple on 10th Road in Juhu. My father came to this temple twice a week at 11.30 a.m. I was present at the same time he generally went. It was 11.28 a.m. I saw old men with wiry sprigs of nasal hair propped up on plastic chairs, women with cane baskets of red flowers, priests in translucent dhotis. I'd seen versions of the scene in the holy town of Nathdwara, where my parents had taken me to the original shrine in my infancy. (I need to say this again for myself: my parents took me on a pilgrimage when I was nine months old.) Standing before the idol – stoically and fabulously black – something skidded in my chest. I hoped no one might notice. I was crying. I'm sure some of the old people at the temple knew me, I thought, and while I have enjoyed a reputation as a difficult man now it was worse: in fact, I was a sentimental one. A small group of women were performing hymns. Their sonorous voices joined to make a sonic crown over my head. I continued to cry, covering my face, until I saw two other pilgrims at the temple – they were also crying! I was suddenly relieved. There were other fools here! They were just like me! They were standing before an idol and crying with folded hands – they were crying for mercy, while I had been crying for grace. And no one at the temple seemed to mind our crying. Perhaps I had not known this simple fact before: we do not go to temples to worship idols or practice faith but to weep together so that our sorrows might be known.

As I stood in the same place my father might have in the same temple, I could feel the space and the song lines that our elders, our ancestors, make and leave behind for us – they carve it out of their feeling for us. One day, without ever knowing it, we inhabit it as our secret inheritance. It's like the doorbell rings one morning and there is a delivery of a suit that fits perfectly; you are no longer naked, you are forever safe, you can arrive at any dinner now. The suit fits you in a way you cannot imagine. It fits you like a glove, or the scabbard for a sword. I was embraced by this feeling that my father had left for me at the temple. In this feeling ran traces of love and hope and gratitude, and a grave, powerful recognition that I had his blood – he had made me. I experienced, all at once, my father's innumerable generosities, his stoic courage and solitude, his sudden, sterling bursts of caring. I remembered he dropped me at school each morning; he kept aside the good reviews of my books in a clear plastic folder; he accompanied me to the dentist's chair as a child. I had never missed my father so much as I did then. Towards the end of his life I would sometimes ask him what he did all day – how he spent his silence – and he always replied, with a big beaming smile, *I am praying for you.*

When we lose an intimate, two deaths occur. The first is the formal, physical death of the person. The other death is of the person we were around them. I reflected on how my father's humour, rage, generosity, petulance and kindness provoked, inspired and shaped me, peculiarly and specifically, for him. I'd been frequently angry around my father. To flesh out our numerous discontents would betray our intimacy. But if fathers have difficult sons it is because they themselves are often impossible. Mine was no exception to this rule, and I was not always pleased with the adult that I was around him: hard, aloof, solitary, irritable, self-contained, sometimes abrasive.

But my father's passing extinguished this particular persona.

I was changed by, and with, his death. My sister Parul said to me that we are as influenced by the presence of others, and of our various selves, as we may one day come to be defined by their absence.

Now I would have to husk aside the person I had been for – and yes, because of – my father. I would have to set aside the learned things. Slowly, with energy, vision and glee, I would have to fashion a new being, one who while reflecting on what has been lost discovers the possibilities of who he is yet to become. Perhaps this sort of thing drove Oscar Wilde to reflect, 'Death must be so beautiful; to have no yesterday, and no tomorrow. To forget time, to forget life, to be at peace.'

There was a great deal to become yet for all that had been my undoing.

––

TWO years after my father's death, I gathered the nerve to return to Jaisalmer, where I had received the unexpected news of his passing. I returned to the same fine hotel, thirty kilometres outside Jaisalmer, in the desert. With my hands on the window ledge of my suite, I gazed out at the same view I had seen when I was here last: an austere flatness of brown landscape. There were lebbek trees; a cluster of cassia. Local wildlife included scorpions, caracal, red foxes, blackbucks. I was not sure if I should experience the calm that I did; I should have felt more pain, or sadness.

There was nothing.

The next morning, I had breakfast. A peacock came to my table for a snack, eyeing the bread basket. This led to the golden retriever – the hotel owner's pet – barking manically. I stood up and went to pet the golden retriever, recalling him from the last visit. He had been standing at the door as I got into the car that would take me to Jodhpur.

'But this is not the same dog,' the retriever's handler clarified. 'This is his puppy. The older dog is gone.'

His words landed on my heart like a stone thrown in a pond; ripples everywhere. On the day I had left for Jaisalmer my sister had alerted me to the kadam tree and its sudden burst of flower, a sweet, magnetic fragrance that dazzled all the bees. Our father had planted the tree even before he built the house; now, long after his passing, the flowers of this tree, bright orange bulbs with delicate white nodules, continued to impart an arresting, sensual perfume. According to legend, Krishna was said to hide in the branches of the kadam tree (also an important, repeating motif in pichwai art). 'The tree must be as old as you,' she had said as I got in the car taking me to the airport in Bombay.

I returned my mind to my breakfast. I saw a turbaned, regal man dressed in formal white walking a dozen domestic ducks. The cool sound of a fountain trickling in the courtyard rang familiar. The peacock, meanwhile, made off with a piece of toast. The desert punishes sentimental recollection.

In Philip Roth's novel, *Exit Ghost*, the protagonist Nathan Zuckerman waits at a restaurant for Amy Bellette, a woman whom he had once adored. Decades have passed since they last met, now she is old and decrepit, beset with brain tumours. But Amy Bellette does not come. An hour later, Zuckerman leaves, fearing that he has mistaken the restaurant where they were scheduled to meet. When he later visits Amy Bellette he finds that the woman who had once held him with the force of her beauty and humour now resembles a madwoman of the streets. After disclosing that her brain tumours have returned and ruined her, she sits Zuckerman down. They discuss a man she had once loved, the writer E.I. Lonoff, also the subject of Zuckerman's lifelong admiration. The book, at this point, becomes less about either of the two living characters, and more about the one who is not there – the ghost between them. Besides, Zuckerman realizes that it was not he who had mistaken the name of the restaurant; it was Amy Bellette who had been incapable of remembering it. When I try and recall my father, as I was trying to do in Jaisalmer, I feel like Zuckerman at the restaurant: waiting for someone who will never come. There was anxiety for the failure of arrival; resentment for being stood up; but mostly shock – for if my father were to join me, I might not even recognize him. That's the awful thing about memory. No, it is not that we forget. It is that we remember differently; we learn *how* to remember: it's a trick of light, yes, but also *of* light. I remember my dad without his fury; I remember him for his kindness to my sisters and me. I remember him for the ghost he has become, not the man he was; he became a character somewhere between Amy Bellette and E.I. Lonoff, living with me in imagination, and yes, outside of time.

–

Evening light in Jaisalmer has a classical golden hue with amethyst undertones. Rain had left a sheen on the flag-stoning that led me away from the hotel and on the dirt track that took me into the desert. Before my walk, I had been watching a segment of the American sitcom *30 Rock* in my room. In a Christmas special, the airy, authoritarian television executive Jack Donaghy – essayed by Alec Baldwin – turns to his deliciously curmudgeonly mother, Colleen (Elaine Stritch is wicked magic) before Christmas and, in a rare outburst of sentimentality, says that he loves her and that he doesn't ever want her to die. Locking her cold eyes with his, Colleen responds almost as if it were a threat: *And I'm never going to*. This is what I needed to hear – an assurance that my parents were never going to die even when they would, and long after they had. Although the task was physically impossible, I see what Colleen might have meant – our folks will always be around.

Why I had returned to Jaisalmer, I had no idea; but what I got out of that trip is something you might know already: that you will go on. My father's death was an insurmountable truth. But with time, its terror had paled to become what it was: a fact, but not the truth. On my stroll at sunset, a memory of my childhood returned. As children, after dinner, my father would insist that my sisters and I walk the long straight length of the compound in our house – to us as kids these walks were deathly dull, although later I would come to see walking as a way of thinking, of airing the mind. On these walks, my father told us stories – *Once upon a time*, he started, *in a magical kingdom, there lived...* Those early stories of animals in the jungle, of escape artists and runaway princesses, of witches and dwarves, were a powerful introduction to story-listening, and a prelude to reading. The cultural historian Marina Warner discovered that in Arabic the root for the word watering – *raawa* – is the same as for a storyteller (*raawi*) and implied that 'narration is irrigation'. My father was out every night, walking his wards, telling them stories, making sure that his garden would one day bloom.

Thank you, Papa, I get that now. I get you now. I hope it's not too late.

Flannery O'Connor believed that as storytellers, and as listeners, we insist on the 'redemptive act' – to observe how what falls and breaks can also be restored. The simple and noble act of listening, and of telling, is in itself restorative, never mind the story. Stories fix us. Stories make us see. Stories remind us how we have failed at love, why we should try harder. Stories teach us when to leave. Stories remind us that we are not alone in our anguish – everyone is a little bit broken, and perhaps better for it. My father's post-dinner stories revealed to me, also, how people care for us in sublime, silent ways, the ways that we don't always recognize or honour in the hour, but which we come to in time.

Slowly, in the wisdom of the backward glance, I came to see – and it was big enough to bowl me over – my father's subtle, nourishing generosities, unacknowledged in his living years, but now so vividly alive to me. I felt lifted and unbreakable thinking that time could turn my past into a book of gratitude, one I had yet not fully read, its surprises astonishing, its denouement always and only love.

On the day my father passed, the sky sheltering us both had been a clean, cold blue. With my mind's eye, I could picture black birds scatter through that cloudless clearing over the fields as I made haste to Bombay – over two years ago – to pay my last respects.

But today there were no birds, the sky was even, clear and excellent.

As I walked back under a gathering night I understood that the birds were neither going home nor coming from it. They had been flying because they could; they were free, after all: ecstatically, if not eternally, free.

———

Bruschetta

In early 2007 a strange thing happened to my father: he went for his usual morning walk on Juhu beach but he was unable to make his way back home.

'I simply couldn't remember where I live,' he admitted in a baffled voice to the friend who later escorted him down V.M. Road, past St. Joseph School and back to our house in Juhu. My father was six feet tall, lean, with unusually long arms, his presence could fill a room; I'd never before have used the word *baffled* to describe his voice, it was more like *clear* or even *terrifyingly clear*.

He was seventy-one years old and, barring a heart stent implant, had suffered no major health issues. At the time of the incident, I was living in a small hill station, Matheran, accessed only on horseback or by foot, densely forested, with abandoned laterite stone mansions. Here birders have seen leopards drag a kill to the branches of a tree near Louisa Point. I was out walking on a remote jungle path, near the Pisarnath Temple, a rough, narrow path through a valley with a steep drop, when my sister called. Our father's physician, Dr Tushar Shah – the only doctor I know who also doubles as a stand-up performer – had advised urgent tests, including an MRI scan of the brain.

An hour later my mother, Padmini, called me and asked me to come back to Bombay. Butterflies of panic billowed out of my mother's voice.

–

As I drove into Bombay, my car paused at the traffic lights in Chembur, near RK Studios, with its emblem of a man cradling a woman in one arm and a violin in the other, drawn from the scene of Raj Kapoor holding Nargis in the 1949 film *Barsaat* (the untutored eye wonders: Is she dying? Is it the ecstasy of a reunion?). The force a dark piece of news carries is in how it makes you question everything – are the trees real, is the sky this leaden grey, was that building always here? Under the Milan Subway is a small marble temple of Sai Baba; a baby, wrapped in a sari, had been found in a garbage dump down the road near Mithibai College. I counted facts of geography and incidents of time to keep truth and fiction from blurring, which occurs in a crisis, even if you have not yet fully entered its mouth. Things were changing, rapidly, secretly, they *had* changed, something in my father's physiology had made him forget where he lived, now he was being wheeled on a stretcher and into the aperture of a giant scanner. The cylindrical bole of the kadam tree in our garden screens out most of the red cement roof of my family house; the flagstoning in our drive was recently redone in grey shahabad stone; I stood in the porch, near a frangipani tree. Before I set foot across the threshold, a few tentative, shielded moments of deceptive calm registered as a kind of grace. In the living room, on a circular glass-top side table, a copy of the *Times of India*, a wedding invitation, my father's reading glasses; the chair he normally occupied – his seat – glaringly bare.

My mother, disabled, enduring bedsores from years of not having walked, of never having left her cot, called out to me from her room.

—

'Of all the cancers,' said Dr Ashok Mehta, a former oncologist with Tata Hospital, 'lymphoma of the brain is a lesser liability.' Dr Mehta and his wife Shirin had been my parents' friends for five decades. My sister Nehal and I had called on him at his clinic in Andheri. Five days after the initial diagnosis we arrived with thick stacks of medical reports. 'Your father will need chemo,' he observed. 'The cancer was caught early on – I am optimistic.' Oscar Wilde believed that 'sheer terror' was at the root of optimism. Personally, 'everything is roses' only ever at a flower show. It was January, mild winter, brackish air, deadly traffic, I was dreaming of the forest, its crown of rui and jambu trees swarming with ghostly white langurs.

Dr Asha Kapadia, lead oncologist at Hinduja Hospital, had a signed edition of a Tyeb Mehta Mahishasura print framed and displayed in her office, a gift from the artist. The occidental accent in her voice was ironed out but you could still pick out leftover traces of smart Manhattan; she had served at New York's Memorial Sloan Kettering Cancer Center for years before moving back to the city of her birth. 'It's not easy,' she said, looking at the test results. She had a cool, steady gaze, she wore crisp cream saris with red borders – vintage Kala Niketan, second floor – and she had probably seen so many people perish that she no longer viewed death as life's coda but as its invisible parallel track. Death was something that happened and happened, and then happened some more. 'Cancer is not easy.' Later, the talented and compassionate Asha and I would become friends, good friends; at the time, I thought her brilliant but formidable, like a sword. Her treatment protocol ultimately cured my father, a regimen so perfect he never suffered a relapse. 'High dose methotrexate would reach the brain and kill the cancer cells. Leucovorin calcium is the rescue medicine that follows – it protects other normal cells and prevents toxicity.' This protocol was administered to my father every two weeks for four cycles followed by two cycles of ARA C – cytarabine – another potent cancer drug.

On the fourth day after his second round of chemo my father sat in his bed, legs folded, howling from pain, like a kicked cur. His white blood cells hovered at or under 700 neutrophils; his mouth had blown up with ulcers. 'You can admit him,' Sunita, an assistant to Dr Kapadia, told me over the phone when I said that my father was in a *state of agony*, a phrase I'd picked up from my mother, who sometimes described her life so. 'We can administer him pain killers in hospital.' But the prospect of returning to the ward, to a white metal bed away from home was such anathema to my father that he simply sat up in his bed at home, clutched his midriff and sobbed, trying to weep the pain out of him. From a black Bose speaker that I positioned by his bedside poured forth Karsh Kale's 'Milan', hypnotic synths and drones under a masterful tabla recital by Zakir Hussain, a track suggesting the meeting of two rivers. The music covered him as if a sheath. His crying tempered, his hands extended up in the air, his head bobbed from side to side, with half a smile; if there was no smudge of blood on his lower lip, he might pass for someone at a classical music concert. Instead, he looked like he was sitting up in a car wreck where, magically, the stereo was still playing. Music, prayer, boxing bags, alcohol (for us), shooting galleries, morphine, walks, hash, therapy, shouting matches – there was no end to the analgesics. In every house where someone has cancer is a wall that's taken a few head knocks. Like a hand running the length of his back, music consoled my father, settling into the tributaries of his pain. When he broke into a smile, my sister Nehal cried from relief.

Meanwhile, my mother was downstairs, in her room, in her bed.

A year after my father was diagnosed, she would go into septic shock and die.

The sky falls. But there are other skies behind it.

You just can't see it at the time.

——

OCTOBER 2009 – eighteen months after my mother had died – I was scouting the net to buy a dresser. An odd, desperate classified: a college student, unable to care for an eight-week-old miniature dachshund puppy, had put her up for adoption. The student arrived at a friend's office in Khar with the puppy, who had the swift, elusive air of a mongoose; tan, brisk, soft, supple as if drawn out of hot wax. Under the shade of a giant rain tree, I rang my sister to say I was coming home with a puppy, she might cheer my father up – he was now cured of his cancer. In early 2008, we had shut off my mother's room after her death; now, we'd have to open it up again, the puppy needed space. On the ride home I felt I was bringing home a baby, her large wondering eyes gazed out at me, her paws were the dearest thing. She had that biscuit smell of puppies.

'Why Bruschetta?' My sister Parul, who met us at the front door, asked. I'd spent the previous summer in Rome where, at a ristorante on the Tiber in Trastavere, a plate of bruschetta was all I could afford on a night out. 'Small but delicious,' I told Parul, who stroked Bruschetta's pendant ears. Behind her, emerging through the hedge of areca palms, a black butterfly with red wing tips.

Although dachshunds were originally bred to hunt badgers, they have also privileged artists and writers as muses: David Hockney's Stanley and Boodgie became subjects of his paintings, and later, a book – *Dog Days*. E.B. White wrote of his own wiener dog Fred, famously recalcitrant and single-minded. For *Vanity Fair*

Dorothy Parker was photographed with Robinson, who exhibited a dachshund's housetraining woes at the Algonquin Hotel – their carpets never recovered. Andy Warhol often arrived at Studio 54 with Archie. Like the artist, Archie was said to stare intently at guests without further comment.

Maybe dogs know this trick, a sleight of paw as it were, they can hack into our loneliness, pry it open like a lock, decode its inner machinery, lay it bare, make us believe we were never teetering into the wrong side of alone. You are on an armchair, reading the newspaper, soles rough from use, widowed heart, clogged veins, chemo fog, long day, longer night. Loneliness is a cave of bats that come out at you each evening, a great black musty whoosh that suggests abject isolation can be a form of purgatory. Old age is a suit of defeats; medals no longer hold – the wars blur. Then a puppy sniffs at your ankle, gingerly, auditioning for a lifetime of loyalty. A whisper from the sunny side of your heart, it all starts to make sense – why Cat Stevens wrote a song, 'I Love My Dog'. In Homer's *Odyssey*, transformed by his travels, their adventure, fatigue, surprise and spiritual nourishment, Odysseus is disguised and unrecognizable. Only Argos, his dog, knows who he is – he sees him as he always was. Milan Kundera believed dogs were our link to Paradise. 'They don't know evil or jealousy or discontent. To sit with a dog on a hillside on a glorious afternoon is to be back in Eden, where doing nothing was not boring – it was peace.'

My father experienced some version of this peace after

Bruschetta had settled into our house. 'Every morning,' he said to me, 'I must say hello to her.' My father was so tall and strong; even after the rounds of chemo, he never lost his hair. 'Before I have breakfast, I must give her one half of my Parle G biscuit.' Sprawled at his feet, she whimpered, recumbent from joy. Falling to his haunches, he tickled her brisket, using the length of his large tapering hands, their suffering saint's slenderness muddling into this soft brown minx of a thing; they were at opposite spectrums of time.

My father was in the veranda when I made the first photo of this odd duo. My father is seated on a plastic white chair, a white bib draping his knees; a barber is shaving his cheeks, his head dramatically tilted back. Bruschetta is watching him through the white metal grill doors that separate the house from the veranda. I am behind her, watching her watch him. She has the air of Tagore's heroine Charulata, domestic, persevering, divided, ruined by love havoc. The true pleasure of a dog's company lies in an exchange of meaningful quietness. Past the tableau of my father with his barber is a square lawn, a line of palms, one large kadam tree with its golden, insanely fragrant flowers in unseasonable blossom. The photograph fails to capture so many things, including the fragrance of the kadam flowers, how my father and Bruschetta exchanged glances – everything gets away, and it's almost always the pretty stuff. In other photos I see Bruschetta watching my father reading the newspaper, or sitting at the opposite end of the couch. Making these photographs was evidence of my father's unusual tenderness for her, which seemed hidden behind his flashes of whiplash anger, his most striking quality from when we were children. And yet, here he was, so uncommonly gentle with Bruschetta, treating her with the honourable reverence usually reserved for a religious artefact. It made me wonder that a kind of diffidence lay behind my father's anger, and that if we had gone past it, we too might have encountered this pale, delicate quality. All along, he was only trying to confirm his own awkward presence in the world and in our lives, it just came out all wrong, except for Bruschetta, who took him as he was. She was his Argos, seeing him through his disguise, the friend he never knew he might hope to have. For all the ways they humanize us, dogs commit a service that borders on alchemy.

I began in 2011 to photograph the two of them, side by side, or by themselves. Bruschetta became an accidental muse, a friend with an original sense of comic timing, with sudden head tilts, holding me with her ocean eyes. If Bruschetta went to bed one Tuesday night and woke up on Wednesday morning as a person – the Kafka nightmare in reverse – it would likely be someone rather small and very smart, maybe the less accomplished but better-looking sister of Fran Lebowitz ('Sleep is death without the responsibility'). 'The world is your oyster but it is also my urinal' – Bruschetta (who never did nail how to land her tinkle in its trough). Never mind! Like a figure out of an old black-and-white reel of Chaplin, she sat up on her bum and raised her front paws in the air, cycling them rapidly, drawing whoops of laughter from everyone around.

One time I was sick, I think I had the flu, a bit down, cut up, weak and bored, testy under a duvet in my bed. A mournful howl outside my door bore evidence of some great, tragic separation. I opened my door, she strode in, concerned, anxious, looking up, then down, before slinking under my white Jaipur razai. Until the following afternoon, muzzle on feet. I'm bad at intimacy although I believe it's good for other people. But this was something else: *whisperable distance*, I thought at the time, close, with room for separation.

The spiritual master Meher Baba believed dogs clean up the spiritual atmosphere of a place. In a letter to Hannah Arendt, the philosopher Martin Heidegger mused over the metamorphic possibilities of love, concluding that 'we become what we love and yet remain ourselves'. Bruschetta taught me – more than any intimate companion – Gibran's counsel of recognizing the 'moving sea between the shores of your soul'. By noon, however, I was keen for her to leave; I wanted to be alone, truly alone, and I could not share this time even with her. I knew mine was a kind of tragic, always, *always* alone. As she left my room, I sat up, my head hurting. A feeling washed over me that I could never ever be with anyone, I had gone past some lines, I was at a very strange and baffling shore. I didn't know if this was a good thing or not.

—

Obedience never made Bruschetta's resume. Fiercely independent, her pride was fragile, she held grudges. When I lectured her for barking she'd steel herself to look at me, then turn and walk away, as if I had been dismissed, a bore, a pedant, someone who didn't know how to roll reefers, who had never sexted (debatable but still) and watched *The Golden Girls* reruns on YouTube (true! true!). Her self-awareness as someone more than a recipient of admonishments taught me a valuable lesson: what to put up with, and when one must quickly, quietly quit. Having established her sovereignty, she embarked on a relationship of equality. When I chided her, she turned and moped about. When indulged, she rolled on her back, oh, the heaven of being alive, the moment her world made sense to her, here she was, lying on her back, this bowl into which I must pour all my affections.

Bruschetta was an original.

She never wore a collar or went out on a leash. She never came when called – she was a dog but playing the part was beneath her. She played fetch when bored, abandoning her ball midway when something distracted her; her priority was pleasure, not routine. In the morning, she ate grass. I never saw a single flea on her. She had the resounding, confident bark of a Great Dane. Courteous to the vet, she was never friendly with him; she saw him as a service provider. Two attempts at breeding her were unsuccessful, either she was not interested in sex or her suitors were both dismal sexual failures, unworthy of her genetic bounty.

She preferred her own company. Slipping her head through the metal grill in our house, she would, for hours, watch time pass. José Saragamo said the only thing dogs want was for no one to go away. She was watching for who was coming back.

As my father settled into the dull, slow shape of his life after cancer, Bruschetta turned a year old, I moved to Moira (population: 4299), a small, intensely green village in north Goa famous for its local oversize bananas and a substantial population of mentally unsound people. I was at home, finally. But I returned each month to the family house in Bombay and to the glorious havoc of reunion. Glimpsing me from afar, when I was in the driveway, Bruschetta would whine from recognition, then come charging out to the door to greet me, paws in the air, finally lying down in a heap at my feet. Our meetings were so weighed with emotion that she peed. Incontinence signalled uncontainable joy reminding me of Tolstoy's exhortation of 'love as present activity' (as in: *I'm presently peeing from the delight from seeing you again*).

——

A T the traffic lights on S.V. Road, under the pedestrian overpass, I rang the vet's clinic in Khar to check up on Bruschetta's X-ray results – she had suffered sudden wheezing bouts in recent weeks. 'It's lung cancer,' the vet told me over the phone.

It was June 2018. The sky was monsoon grey; the air was hot and still.

He said this slowly, hesitating, his words a spider's web; the more I tried to get through them, the more they seemed to stick. Bruschetta had been me with me for over nine years. 'She doesn't have much time. Maybe six to eight weeks to the end.'

Cancer. Time. End. I repeated the doctor's words in my head. His diagnosis. His verdict. *His edict.* The unchangeable thing, the words a decree, or a curse. Now my car passed a row of fruit sellers, a Ganesha temple, a line of stores where college students photocopied their notes (Laxmi Stationery & Xerox). I thought *she will never recover* – I did not have that novice researcher lurking in most people who begins to google any diagnosis with a steely conviction that they will find a way out of it, they will speak with another doctor for a second opinion, they will get the latest drugs, they will prevail over this unfair, unexpected judgment and come away triumphant. Perhaps looking after my parents for as long as I had – the years of holding heavy medical files under my right arm, the years of making nice with insolent doctors – had sent this inner researcher packing. I was invulnerable to hope. I had come to believe that the worst would happen, sooner rather than later; preferably and fortuitously, it would all be quick. Briefly, I felt it was all right for Bruschetta to die – she would be rid of it, this ovarian picnic called *life*, with its tedious detours, prosaic views, soggy sandwiches, and annoying company.

I arrived home.

The doors opened.

I stood over the veined marble floor.

A long, dramatic stairwell; the double-roofed dining hall.

I was in a strange, familiar place, one I knew inside out.

—

Sixteen months had passed since my father had died. He had slipped away quietly in his sleep in February 2017.

Ten years had now gone by since the death of my mother.

Each new death peeled open the skin over the previous loss. All healing is a tentative grace. A fortnight after my father's death, I wrote these lines:

The Museum of Old & New Losses is a fine place
to spend a Saturday evening –
Look at things gone or taken.
All the lovely people you thought you'd never see again.

In this room – follow me, sir – are your old and faithful
friendships, betrayed by some silly incident.
But restored here.

This portrait is called: No One Truly Loved Ever Leaves You.

And in this gallery – The Gallery of Missed Chances –
are hellos you ought to have coughed up at some smoky bar,
The match you should have written to.
One person can change your life.

Our new floor has an endowment
For Specialty Forgiveness:
for your father and the unsaid things between you;
for the sky that grew rude with rain at your wedding.

Saturday evenings now companioned with shining absences,
You sit at the Museum cafe, you order a coffee,
The world goes by, as if it were the same
But it will never be the same again.

—

Dachshunds are prone to the following cancers: mast cell tumours, squamous cell carcinoma and mammary gland cancer (particularly in unneutered bitches). The lung cancer was a mystery, although environment was an obvious indictment – India has one of the world's worst air quality indexes. According to the World Health Organisation, in 2018, fourteen out of the fifteen most polluted cities in the world were in India. Bombay, where Bruschetta lived, ranked fourth among polluted megacities. 'Ambient air pollution alone caused some 4.2 million deaths in 2016, while household air pollution from cooking with polluting fuels and technologies caused an estimated 3.8 million deaths in the same period,' the report said, drawing on a study period of 2010-16.

Bruschetta was small, her cancer advanced, conventional treatments like chemotherapy were more punishing than palliative. By the end of June, her appetite dimmed. She lost weight, her coat fell away. Thinning flesh betrayed her smart symmetry of ribs, her curved brisket. Nine, she looked older, haggard; although not in obvious pain, she was worn beyond reprieve. A sixteenth-century painting by Giorgione of an old woman is titled '*Col Tempo*', or *with time*, cautioning us youth and beauty fade, decay is truth. Rembrandt was among the few other masters who made realistic, severe, unflattering depictions of age – his own self-portrait is proof of his scathing honesty. When I looked at Bruschetta – her muzzle white, her eyes dim and listless – I experienced this same terrible honesty of time. As a puppy, her adorable quotient was out of the park, but now she was leaving us in the harrowing clarity of what happens *col tempo*.

—

I'd read research on how plant-based medications can help alleviate the unpredictable rages of cancer pain, in both humans and animals. A pinch of 'the botanicals' to Bruschetta's diet meant she was back to lounging in my bed. Something of an overnight miracle: her appetite surged; within days her coat regrew. In the lawn, after days of indoor hibernation, she chased after a crow hovering at a black stone bird bath. Even her vet was amazed, although he cautioned me: she is not cured.

Watching my mother suffer from sepsis and die and my father battle the debilitating effects of chemotherapy had left me with one instructive lesson: we can't save the ones we love, but we can try to turn down the volume on their pain. Through our friendship, Bruschetta privileged me the same consolation: by being in it, she rendered my life infinitely less painful. While stroking her, some nameless ache inside me dissolved. The defining aspect of our friendship: we minimized for each other that indefinable, persistent pain defines the condition of being alive.

In November 2018, I published a new book, *The Rabbit & the Squirrel*. For a small piece of illustrated fiction, the book enjoyed a generous reception, with a centrepiece event in Bombay, at the National Centre for Performing Arts, where the actors Jaya and Amitabh Bachchan joined me at its reading. After the reading my friends and I, along with the extraordinary Japanese violinist, Mika Nishimura, who had performed on stage with me, had a memorable, quiet meal at a restaurant at the Royal Opera House – nothing, it would seem, could take away from the sheer perfection and grace of the evening. But the very next morning, I heard Bruschetta breathing with great effort. The scans and the blood work from the last few weeks suggested the cancer was advancing. And now the sound erupting from her had a plaintive, despairing siren, a peculiar, powerful anguish, a call to the heavens, a dry, rasping sound with the clear echo of death – she sounded as if she were being choked. In my panic I called a neighbourhood vet in Juhu – we had initially consulted with him for the first few years of Bruschetta's life before moving her case to a more experienced vet with a larger set-up, including an X-ray facility and lab. When I told him she was suffering – *she is dying, she may have to be put down this instant, please help, I beg you* – he replied: Why don't you go to the vet to whom you have given your business so far?

–

In the car to the vet, my sister and I sat next to Bruschetta, while a dear friend, Siddhartha, rode shotgun with the driver. The pollarded rain trees in Khar allowed sprays of filtered sunlight, which gave the street leading up to the vet's clinic a bucolic air, as if we were going someplace remote and beautiful. Images from the book event the night before that floated through my mind were quickly replaced by the sight of Bruschetta in my arms, labouring to breathe. Anything wonderful that ever happened to me was replaced by something sudden and awful. I tried to meet her gaze but as we neared the clinic, the gleam in her eyes began to dim. We do not find the meaning of life by ourselves alone, wrote Thomas Merton, we find it with another. Siddhartha, who had graciously flown down from Nagpur for the book launch, turned to give me an encouraging look. I thought of all the funerals he had attended because of me. I was embarrassed to be this powerful magnet of bad luck.

At the vet's clinic, it was over quickly, cleanly.

In death, she offered profound generosity: she reaffirmed how presence is the only real gift we can give another.

At the end, we receive ashes.

They are not condensations of being but a reminder that even fire cannot destroy what has been loved.

——

WE returned from the crematorium in Parel. My limbs ached. I finished a bottle of gin. I slept for two days. I was stoned out of my head. I sat in my bed clutching my stomach. I emailed my agent to cancel two book events the following week in Delhi and Calcutta. 'Tell the festival director that I'm unwell,' I emailed her as I flew back from Bombay to my cottage in Goa. How would I tell the literary festival organizers I was immobilized with grief from losing my friend? 'Let's say I sprained my foot.'

I'd always loved the lines on grief by John O'Donaghue: *You are able to function well / Until in the middle of work or encounter / Suddenly with no warning / You are ambushed by grief.* Even to my own ears, to cancel several work-related events 'because my dog died' had a ring of self-indulgence. But recent research on loss and grieving indicates, not surprisingly, that the death of a pet is no less traumatic than the death of a human. *The New England Journal of Medicine* reported on a woman who had lost her dog. She experienced 'broken heart syndrome', the afflicted experience symptoms that mimic a heart attack.

One of the very few people I had told about Bruschetta's passing was a spiritual elder and my confidante, the American writer Amy Tan. We were separated by around twelve hours of time difference. I would message her in the afternoon. She would always, always respond – even when it was 2 a.m. in Sausalito. After her beloved Yorkshire terrier, Bombo, died, she had wept for three days straight and experienced the same sort of paralysis as I. But I could not tell Tan – perhaps I had been embarrassed to say it – that I had not felt this sort of emotional arrest even after losing my parents. Several months later, on her birthday in February, we shared an exchange over WhatsApp that acknowledged the day but also the losses of friends, our own mortality, and a sense of diminished time ahead of an expanse of the untasted world. 'Death is a reminder,' Tan wrote to me, 'that there's always more that could have been said.'

—

Dear Literary Festival Organizer,
I'm sorry for my last-minute cancellation of your events in Bombay and Delhi and Calcutta. My dog died. I am unable to move. I don't expect anyone to understand. I must step aside. Thank you for inviting me.

I did not send this note. My agent stuck to the party line: I had sprained my foot, I was unable to move. The fiction of good manners.

—

My publisher Hemali Sodhi had lost her Labrador, Simba – her *anima gemella*. When I called her, right after Bruschetta's passing, I ended up hanging up on her, unable to speak any more. 'Shall I get on a flight and come see you?' were her last words on that call. She called back. I didn't answer. Later, I came to see that Hemali hadn't ever really recovered from Simba's passing, and continued to mark his birthday or honour moments they had spent together. This made me think: when do we recover? What line must be crossed, what wound must be camouflaged by skin? Is there a date, time, an omen – a black bird must wheel through the house, perhaps? While discussing the death of her son Slade, the novelist Toni Morrison wondered aloud on what sensible, sensitive thing one could say to someone who is mourning:'What do you say? There really are no words for that. There really aren't. Somebody tries to say, "I'm sorry, I'm so sorry." People say that to me. There's no language for it. Sorry doesn't do it. I think you should just hug people and mop their floor or something.' Her friends who tried to soothe her, managed only to soothe *her* – there was no mention of Slade, the singular focus of this great transition. 'They say it's about the living, it's not, it's about the dead.' Resisting closure, even mocking it, she called it *an American thing*. Instead, she said she preferred what she had: 'Memory. And work. And some more ibuprofen.'

Perhaps the essential job of grief is to restore us to the present moment, which is something that also happens in love, when the present moment is too powerful to leave. When Hemali lost another dog, Jack, she fled her Delhi home for the solitary, healing light of Goa's theatrical monsoon. She emailed me from that time to say she was 'living day-to-day'. Yes, I thought – she was finally experiencing time as it was, without either prelude or postscript. Another friend who had lost his sister told me, 'I no longer know how I feel but I do know that I do.' Emotions ahead of articulation. This gift, of inhabiting the present moment (the future is unimaginable, the past too cruel) while simultaneously swimming through a sea of feeling (regret, joy, anger, betrayal, helplessness) is one of the conflicts of mourning. Perhaps what we encounter in our grief as *this is too much* is nothing but our first, vital encounter with entering our lives in the present, and thereby experiencing the full expanse of our own existence as deep, glorious and absolutely terrifying.

In my recognition of Hemali's loss was the realization of the savage aliveness of her anguish – *when would this die? Perhaps hell is only an absence of love.* Quickly and quietly, my personal world distorted, grief soaked through, things grew exaggerated like Dadaist figures, a pastiche of grotesquerie. An ordinary man at the grocery store took on the look of the devil, his nose curved, now a knifing object. Black hair flowed out of a woman's scalp like poisonous tentacles. Sorrow made me anarchic and grim. In this place, the drumbeat of the living world was deafening.

I had to manage my sorrow, I told myself. I had to make my world cohere again. I decided to step out of the house for dinner. Craving sushi, I arrived at my favourite Japanese restaurant, Sakana, in the village of Anjuna. Everything was before me, all the lovely, little things I loved, salmon rolls, miso soup and ebi tempura, sushi coiled in delicate, delicious mutations. But I could not get myself to eat. I was famished, I reminded myself. My hunger was gluttonous. *You must eat something*, I continued. And yet, such a hunger could not be sated with fine plates of raw fish or sake or teriyaki. I motioned the waiter and asked for another Eight Fingers Eddie beer – I was drinking a dreadful amount more. In his autobiography, the musician Eric Clapton – who had lost his young son in a tragic accident – wrote that the only reason he didn't commit suicide at his lowest ebb was because if he died then he wouldn't be able to drink any more.

On the way home to Moira, we drove along the long dark Assagao main road, with its expensive white houses and large shaded verandas. As I came to Gunpowder – a restaurant whose bar ranked me among its fixtures – Leonard Cohen came barrelling out on my playlist: *Going home without my sorrow / Going home sometime tomorrow / Going home to where it's better / Than before / Going home without my burden / Going home behind the curtain / Going home without the costume / That I wore.* Such songs do not play 'by coincidence' but because we have been collecting them on our playlists, like masks, like ointments in a pharaoh's tomb, like vats of honey, like talismans and charms, rolls of linen and palm oil and natron, locked in a gold trunk that accompany the corpse into the afterlife.

Everything in life is only prep for death.

—

When I dared to tell some friends, they said, 'It's tough to lose a pet, but I know you'll recover.' In their commiseration, a profoundly insulting premise: *I am sure you'll get another dog.* Amy Sedaris said that losing a pet was in fact more painful than losing a human 'because in the case of the pet you were not pretending to love it.' That our friends, dogs or people, are considered easily replaceable, filled me with annoyance and dread. Certain friends dropped off my screen. Death has a way of eliminating people who don't recognize your sorrow. Later, you become unable to see them, either – invisible of their own making. Grief is not a record of what has been lost but of who has been loved. In the end, we weep not only for the death of someone but for the startling question that faces us: what shall we do with the love we have for the deceased? Where will we put it?

Who, now, shall be recipient of the gifts of our hearts?

——

IN 2005, Thomas Wrobel, a psychologist with the University of Michigan-Flint, conducted a study on symptoms of grief and our attachment to pets. Guilt for having euthanized a pet was up there. I replayed Bruschetta's last moments in my head – the rasping sound of her breath, the ghostly rattle from her lungs. Had I taken the right decision? What if the wheezing sound had only been a cough? What if she had not been choking, as I had believed? Had the vet made an error of professional judgment, or even a slip of the tongue? Perhaps she had meant to say: It's something she ate, she's going to be fine. But no, as her stethoscope slid over Bruschetta's chest, her brow had furrowed. A few weeks before, her senior colleague at the same clinic had warned me that the cancer was advancing. 'I think it's time,' the vet had said, sensing Bruschetta's extreme distress. But what if I had moved too quickly?

A few days earlier, Bruschetta had wanted to come up to my room. I had ignored her. She had become sporadically incontinent from the cancer protocol, I was concerned she might wet my bed. But now I thought that I should have taken her to my room; I should have let her lie on the bed, her head on my lap. *I had betrayed her last wishes. I had failed our friendship.* My truest feeling about life is this: when will it all be done? But I cannot put myself down. I cannot euthanize the experiences that deaden me. It's not as easy as going into a clinic in Khar and sitting down with a doctor and putting down money for an injection. When I saw Bruschetta had an out on life, I jumped on it. *For the child will have all the toys the father was denied.*

—

In my twenties I spent some of my time at Meherabad, the ashram established by the spiritual master Meher Baba, who among other achievements coined the memorable phrase: Don't Worry, Be Happy. Located a six-hour drive from Bombay, the area has strong, dry summers, cold Mesa winters, an erratic, scant monsoon. The landscape is mostly flat, with acacias and neem trees; owing to a dwindling water table, there are many wells. Alan Wagner, domiciled at this ashram since the seventies, was a dear friend. I reached out to him one weekend after Bruschetta had passed away. His veranda overlooked fields with oxen tilling the dark, dry earth; a bell around their neck issued sweet companion notes. A neighbour's dog barked. I turned to Alan, seated at a circular wooden table, an oval metal tray with tea, ginger biscuits and cheese sandwiches between us. I told him about Bruschetta's last hours, the euthanasia, how in her final moments my sister Parul sat on a cream plastic chair in the clinic, cupping her face, secretly wondering how many more deaths she would have to see. I had been at Bruschetta's side, as the doctor pricked her once. I was whispering into Bruschetta's ear *Nam Myoho Renge Kyo*, the seed mantra of Nichiren Buddhism. It was over within minutes, I told Alan. 'It was a quiet end,' I said.

Our conversation led us to the idea of karma – one's actions from this life and from previous births that shape and influence the present moment. There is a belief suffering cancels out karma. But – said Alan, with his sturdy elbows on the table – I have come to see that animals do not gain in any spiritual way from suffering – it does not lead to their evolution, in the way that suffering can be transformative for humans. 'It is best for them to go when the pain is unbearable.'

I set down the teacup. Many of the buildings in Meherabad are without any paint, a plain brick façade imparts a sincere loveliness. A main building in the older ashram, reached after a railway crossing, was modelled in part on the famous cloisters in New York, columns around a leafy sunlit courtyard. For me, when I later sat in the cloisters, Alan's words were like a warm golden lamp that is turned on in a dark, hopeless room.

At Meherabad, I had known two other pilgrims, Eric and Heather, an American couple in their sixties. They had originally met in the Bay Area before moving to India four decades ago, around the same time as Alan. In 2009, during a burglary, they were violently attacked. A few weeks after the assault, Eric died from the injuries to his brain. The attack occurred on the day after my birthday – I will never forget it. Heather recuperated first in Pune and later in the States, where her family lives. I met her two years after the attack, when she was recovered enough to meet with friends. She was the same strong, generous, enthusiastic, resourceful person I had known from my days at the ashram. Her eyes shone, as if a mirror in her soul reflected the light of distant suns. If anything, the losses had peeled off layers, exposing finer, elegant layers, she had undergone a rumination whose true answer was silence. I remember Eric telling me that when he first moved to Meherabad he swam in his well in the high summer, he read widely, and that he loved Heather with his every breath, more than he did himself.

My condolence call occasioned a walk through a grove of neem trees that foreshadow her house. In this same house, as she had slept in her bed, someone had tried to bludgeon Eric and her to death. There had been blood on the ceiling, Alan told me. The murderers were eventually found and tried. We walked away from this house as she spoke about her husband, her eyes filling up. 'It is my life's work now,' Heather accepted, 'to be a widow.' To be a widow is to remember, to live in recognition of loss, and to live on in honour of the ones who have gone. When Heather speaks, she sometimes lowers and tilts her head to the side, in deference to the person she is addressing, a gesture so old-fashioned and coy it barely conceals that fine shimmering heart.

—

I AM forty-two.
I am neither old nor young.
I am, in the words of Arundhati Roy describing a character in her book, *The God of Small Things*, 'a viable, die-able age'.

And so now this might be my life's work – to learn that I must be a custodian of memory, of defeat, of regret, of questions that will meet no answer. *To learn how to die.*

In bonsai, two key techniques impart age to a plant: jin and shari. In jin, the top head of a bonsai is deadened, to suggest a lightning strike or a windstorm casualty. This imbues a passage of time, underscoring the tree's endurance in the face of struggle. In shari, another ageing technique, incisions are made into the tree trunk, to create a hollowing. These processes make the plant powerful – storm-worn, warrior-like. My closest friend, Urvashi Thacker, a bonsai cultivator, said the techniques implied that 'in spite of death, the tree wants to live on – it *must* live on.' Trees persist with their dead things which, over time, translate into a kind of stark, startling magnificence. *In spite of death, the tree wants to live on.*

Grief is edifying. It encourages recognition. Slowed by pain, you see farther into things. So now I appreciate Rembrandt more directly as an artist of grief, a man who had lost everyone he had loved, his wife, his mistress, his children. Now I fall more deeply into his work, his understanding of light, his searing, even unflattering honesty in recreation. I see why Philip Glass and his 'Metamorphoses Two' was original base material for the orchestral score he ultimately developed for the film *The Hours*, how reiterating violin notes and skidding piano, as comforting as unsettling, suggest the passage of things, the change of seasons. The great rites honour death as a cornerstone, if they are to serve as a true representation of time. Glass was a cab driver before he became a composer and once gave Salvador Dali a short ride. I can see them in the cab, each man encased in their own particular dark genius, not entirely oblivious of the greatness president in the other.

These deaths have left me with an expansiveness; I see across distances, my intuition is formidable.

Death has made me something of a witch.

—

We are all living, which is to say: time is the thing before the end. This must make us embrace life more powerfully, with will, stamina, cunning and imagination. A part of our job while living is to remember the dead. Memory is indestructible – well, most of the time. You think about someone, and they come glowingly alive before you. In my cottage in Goa is a black-and-white portrait of Bruschetta. Poking her foxy little head out of a white metal grill, she is doing one of her favourite things: she is watching the world go by. It appears she is appreciating her time on this planet with her attention to its details. It appears that she is still alive. 'All photographs are *memento mori*,' wrote

Susan Sontag. 'To take a photograph is to participate in another person's (or thing's) mortality, vulnerability, mutability. Precisely by slicing out this moment and freezing it, all photographs testify to time's relentless melt.'

Years after her death, I finally see, and truly understand, the Bruschetta who is in this photograph, her foxy little head wedged out of the grill, observing everything. I was standing before this photograph, staring her in the eye – I was at the point when this would not cause me to tear up. A skin had come over the cut. In the glint of her eyes I saw mischief, wonder, self-assurance, and a longing that would become her private burden: as the one with the superior heart, she would miss me more, and in deeper ways, no matter who had been first to leave.

I sometimes danced around Bruschetta. This was on the days I was alone, but if I felt like a spot of company, she was always around, at whisperable distance. I'd put on some music and move, move just a little, move gingerly, like the world was ending and no one had any clue, in abandon or with wine glass in hand, dancing with my friend, to a song I adored: 'Los Angeles' by The Midnight. I guess the repeating lines are:

Maybe this is just a dream
And maybe we are still asleep
But I, I will miss you when I'm gone.

———

The House Next Door

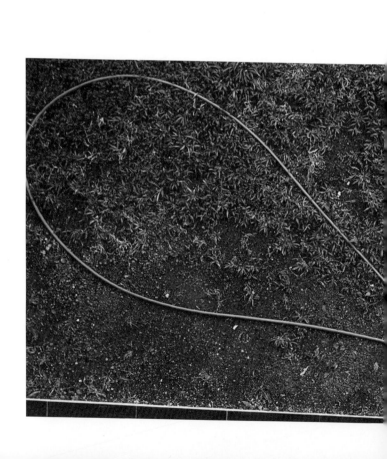

Padmini

Even now, it is as if I were outside myself as I recall the events of that Tuesday, when I had to rush to the hospital and from where I returned home with my mother's body.

A long teak dining table, a chandelier overhead. In a grey ceramic vase: plumeria clusters. Navy linen napkins tucked into uroboros-shaped copper rings; a pale cream tablecloth embossed with a pattern of vines and roses. Two diners face each other – an older woman with waist-length majestic silver hair and a broad, wise brow; a younger man with the slender fingers of a pianist. Viewed through a window, through white sheer curtains, the silhouettes leaning over their plates might be grandmother and grandson.

They are at dinner. It is around 8 p.m. in the third week of January. A lunar eclipse would occur a month later. For an eclipse to take place, three celestial bodies must find themselves in a straight line in their elliptical orbits. This is a syzygy, with its root in the Greek word *súzugos* (yoked or paired). According to Babylonian scholars, eclipses foreshadow the death of the king, who may die during an eclipse, or a month before or after its date. To prevent the king's death, a *šar pūhi* – a surrogate king – is elected, who will die in lieu of the real king, during this astrological upheaval.

My mother was not a king; she was a poet. Yet, sitting at that table that Tuesday evening, where I viewed myself in the third person, I stroked the ancient idea of the *šar pūhi* – the one who is sacrificed.

Could someone else die for you, or could this idea be expanded to mean that you die when someone does?

—

'We must go to the hospital immediately,' said Saraswathi Devi, my godmother. She lived in Berkeley, where she ran a yoga shala originally founded by her guru, Swami Vignananda. But she had flown in a day before from America on a lightning visit after she heard my mother, Padmini, had been admitted to the ICU; among the many spiritual occasions to which she brings intuition, grace and familiarity are childbirths and deaths.

'We must leave now.' She set down the spoon; her plate of moong daal and brown rice had been barely touched.

'Well, we just got back from the hospital.' As I was to spend the night in the ICU waiting room I wanted, at least, to finish dinner in the quiet of home.

But she was not listening. 'Let's go now.' She stood up from her seat, solemn as a spire. 'Ask your sisters to join.'

Saraswathi's words felt like snow falling on my heart.

When I called my sister, Nehal, she said she was just on the phone with the hospital – the resident at the ICU had noticed severe irregularities in my mother's breathing. She had already called Parul, our older sister, who was also on her way to Nanavati Hospital, in north Mumbai. Invisible hands were drawing us to the yellow glow of a night lamp in a hospital room.

As I shut the house door behind me, I recalled the Auden lines:

The unmentionable odour of death
Offends the September night. . .

—

As we drove to the hospital I recalled how, only a few days ago, I had accompanied my mother to the hospital in her ambulance.

Padmini was conscious, but her eyes were tired, and bewildered. *Yet another hospital stay*. To distract her, I pointed to the things she could glimpse from the ambulance window, the evolution and losses of landscape. The Patels' bungalow had been brought down and replaced with a high rise. The local college had a new wing for economics which unfortunately looked more like a mall that might house a worryingly large number of plus-size clothing outlets. A wide selection of hookers paraded outside Nehru Nagar slum. We passed my best friend Urvashi's house, Nirant, a little ways before Nanavati Hospital. So much of life is simply geography – and geography, like life, changes. Wrecking balls bring down factories, squalls take out trees, wars loot out temples, fires consume opera houses, rivers dry up, continents splinter and divide – things go from familiar to unrecognizable. Years ago, I had scribbled in my writing diary a line out of a novel by Michael Ondaatje. *The trouble with all of us is we are where we shouldn't be.* (All reading is a way of encountering your life before you must live it – a poetry of caution.) We are where we shouldn't be, my mother might have thought in the ambulance. And where will I go from here?

In the blinking darkness of the ambulance I accounted all that was still intact, unchanged, prime among them my mother, unbreakable, indivisible, a sage of losses, a graduate (with honours) from the University of Untold Suffering.

'The poinciana trees outside Geeta Ben's house are gone?' she asked.

'Yes,' I said, as I tried to figure how long it must have been since she had left the house without an ambulance. The poinciana trees had been cut five years ago when the road was being widened. In recent years, most of her trips out of home were only to the hospital, always by ambulance. But this was the first time she was taking inventory. 'The flame trees have long been gone.'

She did not say anything, but a look of betrayal came over her eyes. 'Your father and I had planted those trees,' she told me as we entered the gate of Nanavati Hospital. 'We were among the first to move to Juhu, when long stretches were still marshland – it was very rough then, but beautiful. In our early days in Juhu your father and I would buy saplings from the municipal nursery and plant them along the lane. We had planted many of the trees on our street, including the rain trees.' When she held my hand, I felt it was as if she was drowning. The Saint Thomas Christians of Kerala believe a poinciana tree was beside the cross Jesus was crucified upon. His blood smeared on them, imparting memorable and intense colour to the blossoms.

——

I N the late nineteen twenties, my grandmother Rukshmini Divecha proposed to Arvind Vasavada. Two years her junior, he was a fellow student at Wilson College as well as her philosophy tutor. Her mother was supportive of her choice but her father, who had amassed a fortune in the colonial years, was dismissive – the young lovers were not social equals. Rukshmini, however, did not care about either money or status, and perhaps even decried them. A staunch Gandhian, she wore khadi saris that she wove herself and participated in the freedom movement. After a simple wedding, she packed her clothes in two metal trunks and left her family estate, just off Altamont Road, where one of the neighbours had a pet leopard who was walked on Marine Drive. The couple moved to Banaras, where Arvind was posted as a professor with the philosophy department at Banaras Hindu University, then widely considered the 'Oxford of the East'. Here, in a small tin-roofed cottage allotted to academic staff, Padmini was born at the end of one June, inheriting from her mother bright, boundless courage; and from her father philosophical inquiry for the world, its rousing mysteries, its hysteria and dreams, its shattering, sublime truths. Every evening, at dusk, hundreds of small lamps floated over the Ganga, in memory of the deceased, as prayer, in homage to departed souls. The Ganga was the river my mother grew up near.

I can picture floating diyas, lamplight breaking up over rippling sheaths of water. I can picture this clearly, although I haven't seen it myself, for my mother had seen this so often that it was a kind of visual bequeath. The gifts my mother gave me continue to surprise me long after her absence. As I look back, there had been many such other fine exchanges when she had been alive, and which I had failed to credit.

Padmini met my father, Dhanvant, via an arranged marriage set-up. She declined the match after the first meeting. He persisted. She was reluctant to move from Jodhpur, where my grandfather, Dr Arvind Vasavada, was then teaching at university, to Bombay and into a domestic milieu of material riches. Ultimately, at my father's repeated requests, she relented. The match was unusual. My mother came from a sterling stock of intellectuals and thinkers. Her father had exposed her early on to the poetry of Yeats and Shelley, and the literature of the Bengali masters. Even their picnics were animate with lectures on sections of the *Bhagavad Gita*; my grandfather had done his doctorate on one of its more arcane parts – the 'Tripura Rahasya'. In family albums are photos of him with Dr Carl Gustav Jung, under whom he had studied dream analysis in Zurich, with Dr Radhakrishnan, who had mentored him through his dissertation, and with J Krishnamurti. In the acknowledgements of her masterpiece *Women Who Run with the Wolves*, Clarissa Pinkola Estés lists Dr Vasavada as one of her gurus.

My father was the son of a wealthy businessman (his father, Tapidas, an orphan, was a self-made man and in his older years became a Sanskrit scholar, reciting parts of the *Gita* each morning with a student's earnest diligence in the courtyard of

Chandra Vihar, a large white house in Parla, north Mumbai).
My father drove around in a white Fiat; for mysterious reasons,
a previous engagement of his had been annulled; he drank
chilled beer in steel glasses and his oeuvre of sixties' print shirts
belonged in the permanent collection of the Museum of South
Asian Hipsters. My father, for all his life, was a lonesome thing, a
fine friend, a complex family man, a badass smoker. He had large
hands and tapering fingers – that's where I get mine from.

The extended fray of my father's joint family had baffled my
mother. The women had key concerns that included matching
blouse pieces to expensive saris and running a kitchen where
pickled turmeric was one among nine condiments essential
at luncheon. A Gujarati theatre of mediocrities. My mother
was a misfit here, as she nursed neither sartorial nor culinary
ambitions. She wrote poetry in Hindi to shield herself from
domestic trivialities. She read Bengali masters. My father was a
doting, indulgent husband. But even his habit of reciting aloud
to her the lines from T.S. Eliot or George Bernard Shaw could
not diminish his impulsive, implosive rage, a lifelong affliction, a
fire that would torch either out of recognition.

How do people fall in love? By accident, in blindness. Or
do you go through thinking that it might happen to you one
day, perhaps even with the person to whom you are married,
and that while it hasn't yet, it could happen tomorrow, or the
week after? My mother had entered married life in hope, a hope
for communion, of family, and that one day, unexpectedly, she

would fall for her independent-minded, hot-headed husband who took her to see plays at Bhaidas Sabhagraha every Saturday evening. How nice they might have looked driving up to the theatre in a white Fiat, the young couple: the sinuous wife with her luscious hair expertly done in a French twist; the reedy, tall man in a white shirt with a print of music records. No one could see the anger that sat between them like an apparition.

A year after the birth of my sister Parul in 1967, came Utpal.

Utpal was the brother I never met: before he turned four, he fell off a third-floor window ledge and plummeted forty feet down at an aunt's house on Hughes Road. A part of his skull burst open from the impact. The end was sudden, tragic, devastating, a great upheaval, an act of God, the sort of thing that can drive you mad. In his childhood photos he looks angelic, so beautiful that the only honourable thing was for him to perhaps die for his beauty. Angelic, as if he had been born auditioning for the part, an amateur seraph. Sonal Shukla, a family friend, recently told me she had a memory of little Utpal breaking from my father's clutch and rushing across the main road, ending up on the divider at the mid-section from where he began to sing 'Mere sapno ke rani'. His musical prodigy was marked.

Raphael painted the Sistine Madonna in 1512, using malachite mixed with orpiment and vermilion, words that sound like the ingredients of a spell. While it is impossible to unglue your eyes from the Madonna in her dramatic blue robe,

Saint Sixtus on one side, Saint Barbara to the other, there are two winged cherubs at the base of the painting, resting on their elbows. The cherubs' expression is gloriously bored – what am I doing here, it seems to ask, as if the painter were mocking us for our serious gaze, deflecting from the religious solemnity by coiling art in humour. In many of Utpal's childhood photos, I see a similar deadpan expression, a child's undecorated boredom. *What am I doing here?* I have a blue shirt he wore, among the last ever made for him by my mother's tailor in Vile Parle. The shirt is lovely, the last button missing; it reminds me of the line – *the smallest coffins are the heaviest.*

After my sister Nehal, I was born. By then, my father was forty, my mother in her mid-thirties – four kids, three alive, two miscarriages. I guess if we all listed our losses we'd seem like a catalogue of ruin. And I guess if we knew what is going to happen to us later, we wouldn't even bother to start out.

—

When I turned five, my mother began to complain of pain in her legs. Her calves hurt; her joints were reddened. Soft slow pain, like a hymn at a funeral.

The family physician, Dr Himanshu Shukla, made an initial examination. He reported to Sonal, his wife: 'I just hope it's not rheumatoid arthritis.' But tests and investigations confirmed that it was. A vile, ravenous, advancing disorder that ate into my mother, inflaming joint after joint – I imagined it like a giant squid that swam through the dark sea of her flesh, pulling in, flashing out, glamorous, venomous. Even the surgeries to replace her knees, and later her hips, did nothing to slow the decline, or crush the agonies that rose out of her, the smouldering lava of pain. Virginia Woolf lamented there was an inadequate selection of words for pain. 'There should be cries,' she wrote, 'cracks, fissures, whiteness passing over chintz covers, interference with the sense of time, of space; the sense also of extreme fixity in passing objects; and sounds very remote and then very close; flesh being gashed and blood spurting, a joint suddenly twisted – beneath all of which appears something very important, yet remote, to be just held in solitude.'

Growing up, I watched Padmini hobble around the house, then use a cane stick which was later replaced with a metal walker. A black creaking wheelchair was prelude to the few years before she became entirely bed-bound. I designed a mobile bed for her along with the carpenter Ramshakal. This wooden bed, with its black industrial trundles, wheeled her out of her bedroom now and again, especially for the launch of her book of poems that came out in the last years of her life. In the attic, her walking sticks, her walker, her two wheelchairs – all the useless things. Outside her window, on a green grill, the Rangoon creepers bloomed wildly. She spent her time looking at the flowers bloom and wither, bloom and wither. She had printed the book of poems herself; my favourite in this tiny collection is 'Bhatkan' or *Wandering*, written in the early years of her marriage. A woman advises herself to steel against the original, universal laments of time; this poem has the raw, enduring quality of something perfect chanced upon by an amateur. It is whole and perfect, without artifice, possessing a private, sweet sound corralled with ache.

—

Y mother was in her mid-twenties when she experienced, at close hand, two deaths: the death of her mother and her son.

After Utpal's demise, she moved to the town of Pune to mourn; she lived in a two-bedroom apartment near the racecourse. Her handwritten letters to my father, who was back in Bombay, were dazed and anguished; she was a young woman flung out of herself. A snake might look at its moulted skin and wonder: what is that? But slowly, with language, she reconstructed the broken pieces of herself; the letters helped. My father built a new house, where they would ultimately settle, and where I was later born. Her letters from Pune were about the difficult, messy business of grief, but they equally gave voice to her longing for my father. I found the letters complicated, even contrarian. They radiated romance (although most evidence indicated that the temperaments of the writer and the recipient were utterly mismatched).

I once asked my mother how she came to be at peace with the loss of Utpal, her second child.

'I had returned from Pune after a long stay there. Your father had built a new house in Juhu, to where we had moved, a house by the sea. One afternoon, I was cooking when a sadhu came to our doorstep. He asked the maid if he could meet with me. I was reluctant but he said he would not leave until he had met with me. His long, matted hair was rolled into a bundle on top of his head – he looked more like a hippie than a sadhu. He explained he was not looking for money but that he had a message for me. I

was intrigued. He asked if I had recently lost a child. I was shocked
– how could he know about Utpal? Then he asked me when I had
lost my mother. I said it was in1968, November; a year before, in
October, Parul – my first child – had been born.

'The sadhu said that my mother was desperate to spend more
time with Parul. Sadly, she died when Parul was only one. But
her burning desire to spend more time with Parul persisted.
According to the sadhu, Rukshmini Divecha was reborn as
Utpal; in this avatar, she spent three years with Parul and with
me. When the spirit was contented, the body dropped. The
sadhu did not want me to view Utpal's death as the death of my
son but as a kind of continuing relationship with my mother.
There was no evidence for me to believe him. But after he told
me what he had, something in me sealed up, a tap twisted shut.
I never again mourned, or missed, Utpal. Over the years, my
heart lifted as I imagined my mother had had the closure that
she had needed.' Her voice was elated – a puddle of sunlight –
before trailing off. I wondered if she was using this to explain
Utpal's death to herself. States of deception rely on the intensity
of despair. The fiction we tell ourselves must be more refined –
more compelling – than the fiction we make up for the others.

To me the sadhu's explanation was simplistic, naive,
unverifiable, rooted in either ignorance or desperation. When I
said as much, my mother pointed to her father's studies in rural
Rajasthan – research on people who claimed to have been reborn
and had very accurate and damning recollections of their past

life. A woman in Bhilwara who had drowned herself was reborn in a village a hundred kilometres away, where she grew up; in her present avatar, she identified the men who had caused her to commit suicide in her previous manifestation: she knew their names and the torturous incident that had led to her death. There had been many such instances of children detailing their past lives with shocking particulars from their previous manifestation.

While I remained sceptical of my mother's explanation, I knew it had given her courage, dressed the wound, led her weeping to a pasture. A few years later I read again Karen Blixen's *Out of Africa*. I recognized its cultural stereotyping, its gratuitous exotifying. But the aesthetic merits overshadow its shortcomings, and the memoir throws into sharp relief the idea of nostalgia as grief. By the end of her long term in Kenya, Blixen had endured numerous tremendous losses – of friends and faith, of a marriage, and of a beloved life-giving farm. A week after the tragic death of her lover, Denys, in a flying accident, she begs the universe for a sign to give her suffering a shred of meaning, a purpose or a reckoning. On a walk through her farm she spots a chameleon and a rooster. When the chameleon sticks its long, threatening tongue out at the rooster, the bird plucks it out. Certain that the chameleon would not be able to fend for itself without its tongue, she takes a stone and bludgeons it, putting it out of what might have been slow, anguished death from starvation. This is the reason, she tells herself, that she had been sent to Africa at all – to help contract the suffering of one creature. 'When in the end, the day came on which I was going away,' she wrote, 'I learned the strange learning that things can happen which we ourselves cannot possibly imagine, either beforehand, or at the time when they are taking place, or afterwards when we look back on them.' A little incident, entirely disconnected to the larger, more flamboyant chronicle of her life, helps her put her house in order; she is, now, ready to leave and rebuild her life. And on her return to Denmark she begins to write seriously ('no one came into literature more bloody than I' – Blixen used this phrase to describe her late flowering as a published writer at the age of fifty).

Whether I believed my mother's reasons for how she resolved the end of Utpal's brief life – and the great event of his death – I recognized that she was doing this simply to stay alive: she was telling me, and herself, a story to link that great and perplexing invisible distance between life and death. Narrative was her secret ladder to order the realms. Perhaps the ancients were wrong to assume a river divided the living from the dead: a mythic river that was churning and roiling, a liquid coil of furtive depths and crazed rages, infested with horned and tailed beasts that must be fought and conquered.

Perhaps the ladder between life and death was simply one rung silence, one rung word.

This is how we go.

This is how we cross.

––

Y mother's acceptance of Utpal's demise revealed the powerful link between language and resolution, of how we darn tiny pieces of fiction into the larger fabric of our lives, *to keep it all together*. As her health began to restrict her movement, my mother imparted to me instructions for the writing life, without ever meaning to. While we had to attend functions in the extended family – Diwali lunches or weddings or birthdays – she remained in bed. On our return from the gatherings, she insisted on a graphic retelling of the event. Was the shrikhand as delicious, loamy and saffron-infused as she remembered? Was the obese alcoholic cousin, who had wed his own manly sister-in-law, exonerated from the domestic violence charges brought on him by his first wife? Our family tales were like a seedy tele-novella, an episode of *The Bold and the Beautiful*, except everyone was bald, and Gujarati, and property battles replaced sexual intrigue.

At first, I told her what I remembered of these tedious functions – clothing, decoration, food; how everyone spoke about cricket, marriage or weight loss. *The Ugly*, I told her once, *Are Now Uglier*. But she didn't want bitchy commentary, or reports on serious lapses of intelligence; she wanted a tidy black box of masala anecdotes. As I grew older, I began to amplify incidents, ornament prosaic events, edit out fatty trivialities until the thick residual broth of anecdote was complex and nourishing. Like a weasel delights in its dance, my mother did in my details. The dormant part of her life now ran alongside my observations, limber as a whippet on lure. This performance of storytelling was a vital apprenticeship for a writer's trade: to observe, recall, revise, to tell a story without lapsing into the predictable, marshalling forward with juice and sparkle, allowing for pause as well as the swift, sudden swerve. When an aunt at these functions said to me: Look how you have grown! I mouthed to myself: *And you have too, you have grown and grown, and it is now time to stop.* I hurried home with adolescent scraps of banister wit for my mother, who laughed her heart out, and briefly it seemed her many miseries grew silent and her laughter was louder than her sorrow – louder than all life.

From my mother I learned a writer had to immerse her mind in a world so different from her own that she might, briefly, forget it; or forgive it, especially when she saw other worlds came with other cruelties.

To write was to help someone else erase some part of their pain. It was as simple as that.

This was the first motive for all my writing. It remains so.

–

The quality that advances writing – the physical act of publishing something truthful and, therefore, incendiary – and the process of thinking about the writing, about raising the difficult questions and enduring impossible answers – relies on courage. My mother was courage in motion. When I was around nine years old, seven dacoits invaded our house brandishing knives and village pistols. The terrified watchman clasped on to a part of his upper lip torn apart in a bloody scuffle; then, the dacoits tied us all up with ropes and robbed our cupboards. My mother, entirely calm, instructed the dacoits about what they could take and what they should leave; oddly enough, they paid her mind. Some months later, this gang of robbers was apprehended. In a police identification parade, she singled out one dacoit. He was 'the guy who *didn't* take her diamond earrings' after she had said they were her mother's wedding gift to her. Go easy on him, she requested the investigating officer.

My father had spent his life savings to build a school in memory of Utpal, my deceased brother. A sprawling concrete building, a large football ground (where I sometimes hid when bunking algebra), the school was flanked at its rear by the ISKCON Temple. On the annual day of this north Bombay school, the student body wanted to present my father a bouquet of flowers on the stage. A trustee objected to this show of gratitude towards the school founder. My father, keen to dodge controversy, stepped back. But my mother took the trustee to the green room. 'See my shoes?' She dangled one of her patent black leather mules before his face in the green room's harsh light. 'I could thrash you to an inch of your life right here, or I can do it once we are on stage.' The school kids presented my father a bouquet without incident.

Her courage, in some of its refractions, was female – and feminist. At Sahakari Bhandar in Juhu – in an era when the home store still sold white Bata canvas school shoes – a sales clerk was nasty with my sister Nehal, a child at the time. She began to cry. Seeing the power dynamics at play – an adult male terrifying a little girl into tears – my mother accosted the clerk in the store manager's room, and gave him an unforgettable dressing down. She spoke so tall and clean and fierce, the girders might have quavered.

My sister Parul was frequently hospitalized as a child. Padmini began to see through the charade of doctors who insisted on expensive, painful test after test simply to rack up revenue for the hospital. She was not going to put her six-year-old child through another invasive and unnecessary test only so some doctor could make petty cash for his employers. The specialist then made a threat – my sister would lose a kidney if she didn't get an urgent test done. My mother looked the specialist in the eye before throwing a file of his bogus test papers at his face: I'll kill you before *that* ever happens, she screamed. She stormed out of his cabin and that same evening she moved Parul out to another, better hospital where she made a full recovery.

I saw my mother's courage at home, when she spoke to my father in the same high, fuming tones as his. One night, when Sonal Shukla was at our house, my father was at the dinner table, dining alone as he preferred on a long, lonely table with a formica top. For no reason, his temper flared. The uproar about the food – the daal was under-salted, the chapattis too chewy – had the strains of his usual menace. My mother left Sonal's side in the living room, went past a wooden screen and reached the table, where she upended his entire plate of food – if the food she had made for him was not up to scratch, he had no reason to eat it. The brilliant Sonal, whose pioneering firebrand activism shaped feminist discourse in India, would have overheard the exchange – this domestic squabble, and the power levelling by one woman who was valourizing equal rights by insisting on them for herself.

Goya's sketch of Agustina de Aragón depicts an imposing woman of tall, full form in plain domestic attire. Clothed in white, standing over dead soldiers, she is lighting fuses that release cannonballs on advancing French troops at the Siege of Saragossa in the 1800s. A muse to Byron and others, Agustina was said to be an ordinary girl who discovered her more valiant side as an opposer to war. Unlike previous expressions of courageous women in art, which celebrate dramatically robed warrior queens, or goddesses with many hands, the simplicity of Agustina's attire – her peasant woman threads – hints that a domestic woman can be an army unto herself. I imagined my mother in the manager's room at Sahakari Bhandar, her hand over her daughter's shoulders, teaching her how to stand up to men not simply as an act of self-preservation but as her birthright.

One thing my mother taught me early on: the dinner party does not always have to go on.

––

IN 2005, Prince Charles married Camilla. Katrina ambushed New Orleans. Tiger Woods won his fourth green jacket. Parveen Babi died. Delhi was rocked with bomb blasts. Around this time, in Bombay, I had begun to attend parties, which was entirely out of character for me – I had been a lifelong hermit. But the success of my first novel, *The Last Song of Dusk*, led to unnecessary, exciting invitations. I was in my mid-twenties, surprised by sudden popularity, and happy to go. But after the second drink I realized something was radically amiss – I simply did not belong here among this gilded set of private jet owners and art collectors; the hours spent on such long dinner tables registered as seismic shock to my spirit – invisible, powerful jolts. Knocking back vodka as if water, I'd return home furious with myself for making small, stupid talk about classic restaurants in Corsica and whale-watching safaris off the Mirissa coast. I felt deeply estranged from the shy, soulful parts of my imagination that had been a shell for my writing. It was late when I returned home from such shindigs, long after midnight, and I would peep into my mother's room. Invariably awake, she would ask what was bothering me. I'd sit next to her and, without any irony, tell her that folks I had met were all breaking neat lines of cocaine with black credit cards, their chit-chat was insipid, they were insincere and insecure. I expressed woes of my extreme privilege to a woman who had watched helplessly as her second child tumbled out of a window to his death, who had emerged from the crash of a vexing marriage with more than a few nicks, who was now strapped to her bed, unable to move left or right without assistance, who sometimes called out in agony in the late afternoon, a peculiar arresting desperate sound, like a whale trying to revive a dead calf, circles of grief expanding into the cold blue of sky.

And yet, she would comfort me.

She would remind me I was lucky to be invited. She told me to enjoy my fame but to never quite believe it. Write more. Read, read, *read*. Sometimes she would sing something, a bhajan, a lullaby. I'd make her masala chai which she would drink in small gulps from a plain white tea cup. The atmosphere, before dawn, had an amber attic darkness where meaning, truth, regret, insight changed hands like rare coins, every word of hers a salve to my wound.

She would ask for water. She would breathe, slow, laboured.

We would resume our talk.

As she would speak, a part of me would wonder: did the great grief of Utpal's death slide into my mother's bones? Did it seep into the cavities in her joints and inflame her able knees with death's illimitable reserves of sadness? Did death wreck a young marriage, divest it of all its clean bone-white hope, and its tact too? What else dies out with the one we lose? If Utpal had lived, would her marriage, and her health, been happier or better? It wasn't as if only my brother had died: with his death, many other things had shuttered permanently. These questions volleyed back and forth, without resolution; the only solace was conversation – the recognition of sorrow ahead of language, yet one that might be soothed only by words. Why do terrible things happen, I would ask. She would wonder aloud: was her suffering a karmic backlog – activity from previous lifetimes – that she was living out now? Or was her illness only something unfortunate and inexplicable and awful, no reason, no end, as random as rain? What could pain teach any of us? Was it not possible that joy might teach us the same lessons but without the anguish? Why was suffering considered instructive, or illuminating, but not pleasure?

Breathe. Let it go. Let it be. Nothing mattered. It was all an illusion.

Later, I saw our questions were the stuff of books we had read and re-read: Munshi Premchand and Saratchandra Chattopadhyay in her case, Toni Morrison and Virginia Woolf in mine. Woolf was surprised pain was never considered a serious subject, as vital and urgent as war or fate. She wrote an essay about the subject, 'On Being Ill'. Perhaps she believed pain was egalitarian and unifying, in contrast to joy, which remained rare, a dispensation. To talk about life was to talk about books, and to talk about books was to talk about how we are alive, and essentially how we are punished or why we have been rewarded. In *Godan*, Premchand writes – *what the world calls sorrow is really joy to the poet*. Was it so for Padmini? When I read the literature around death and grief – memoirs from talented Western writers – I marvelled at their clinically precise language, the thrilling force of saturnine curiosity, their intellectual range to locate, identify and describe the electric physicality of pain, how they verified and examined loss, like a frog on the dissection table. But when the world of pain was taken apart, no one knew what to do with the pieces. These exquisitely written and often deeply moving books did not tell me what I had to accept: things happen because they happen. But *why* any of it happened, why someone was picked to have their brain opened up in surgery while another – the pillion rider on the same bike, that night the awful accident happened – got off with only a nick and a cut... There was no answer. As in a novel of Marquez, fate enjoyed incorruptible superiority. Some of us had such good deaths, surrounded by the ones we loved, at home, in bed, silently, after eating strawberries and fresh cream, after saying thanks and farewell. The pipe had been smoked. Some of us had awful deaths, the kind whose wailing and flailing we shall never forget. You want curtains, not a car crash.

But who decides who gets what sort of end?
Nothing mattered. It was all an illusion.

——

A T the tail end of the nineties, my mother introduced her dentist to a yoga instructor, a woman of breathtaking plainness. Like the dentist, the yoga teacher had long been single and both possessed a matching spinsterish air. After a brief meeting had been set up, in which each recognized the other as an equal in loneliness (and social defeat), they wed. My mother's many attempts at arranged marriage had been heroically unsuitable but this one was special; it had a karmic backlash. Soon after the marriage, the dentist came to see my mother, where an admission of married life as *difficult* quickly led to a full-blown disclosure: the yoga teacher had announced celibacy vows. Redolent of mice, the antechinus is a tiny marsupial from Australia that often mates with females of the species with such stamina and rapidity that corticosteroids swell dramatically in its blood stream. This suppresses its immune system resulting in its death, from a sexual activity called synchronous mating, basically death from sex, something the dentist would *never ever* achieve. You could almost hear him clawing on the walls, like an asylum inmate.

As my mother's age caught up with her, she required dentures. The dentist volunteered. My mother didn't wish to suffer full expense so she booked a partial denture on her lower front four teeth. Her proposition of thrift failed to account for the outcome that now she would be able to scare little children simply by smiling at them. The dentist made my mother's dentures glaringly white – 'widow white' – and they glinted from her mouth. Compared to her original timeworn teeth, they had a slightly terrifying air, like fangs. The dentures were ill-fitted and fell out of her mouth often. Once at a funeral, while commiserating with the widow, her dentures jumped out of her mouth and wedged into her sari blouse. 'Excuse me,' she said to the visibly horrified woman who had just lost her husband four days prior. Diving into her blue cotton blouse she plucked the four fake teeth out and fixed them back over the track of her gums.

In my eighth grade the teacher called her in for a joint meeting with me, after having written in my report card that I had an 'acidic tongue that alienated me from my peers' – perhaps the only accurate thing someone said to me before the age of sixteen. I had also failed chemistry, perhaps because the only thing I wanted to do as a troubled adolescent in the lab was blow up my peers with their Bunsen burners. The teacher believed it was time to have a 'talking to' with my mother about her socially retarded and bookish son. As my mother began to defend me, a Denture Moment ensued: her teeth flew out of her mouth and landed on the teacher's lap. Shrieking as if she had been assaulted by a mugger in an alley, the teacher appeared stricken. I rubbed my palms over my thighs, unable to contain my glee. Never again did the teacher call in my mother, although this would have become physically impossible: a year later, Padmini began to use a wheelchair to get around and our school had no ramp back then.

But my mother's ill-fitting jack-in-the-box dentures were not the dentist's only revenge for his arranged marriage from hell. Before I turned sixteen I had been to the dentist so often that I no longer read our magazine subscriptions at home. I had enough hours to fill in the dentist's cabin, where the wall art was framed photos of decaying teeth and cancerous gums. Every other week I was called in to fill a cavity or endure a root canal. Caps were made. Braces were suggested (I was well past the teenage brace years). Tartar was removed, then removed again to be safe, and yet again for good luck. 'You might have gum disease,' he said, his drilling gun against his right temple. I stopped going to the dentist. I decided I would let all my teeth fall out, or maybe I'd allow one to remain, and it would grow out of my mouth like a tusk, a sight sure to enchant my future lovers.

My father too underwent an endless series of dental procedures that might, in retrospect, serve as a cautionary tale against organizing arranged marriages. My father's dental work never ceased. He was at the dentist's every week. He might have even died there, on the black leather reclining chair, after another painful filling. None of this stopped my mother, who continued to set people up, and she did this even out of her bed. Even as she was being vandalized by pain, her conviction in the vivid potentials of love – that no one needed to go through this alone, this awful, tormented, mostly pointless life, without the animating pleasure of conversation at the dinner table – was a noble, wild thing.

—

Nan Goldin's *The Ballad of Sexual Dependency* is a series of biographical photographs, of self and of tribe, reflecting an eighties' era of hard drugs, cheap lust and rock music. The pictures vibrate emotion, with the heartbeat of a particular time where death was common – from overdose, from AIDS. Looking back on her 35 mm pictures of lovers in bed or embrace or breaking up, Goldin reminisced: 'I used to think that I could never lose anyone if I photographed them enough. In fact, my pictures show me how much I've lost.' My mother never thought like this about love. She never imagined its end, she never counted her casualties, and her desire to champion it to others made me wonder if she saw love as an antidote to death.

And from where exactly did she derive this facility for hope in love?

As a teenager, I once came home from school to see her feet immersed in a tub of leeches, palliative leeches, trained to suck the 'bad blood' out. I was too young then to know the extreme measures my mother had embarked on after her hip and knee replacements did not diminish her suffering or make walking pain-free. When I was looking at Goldin's photos I immediately thought back to my mother with her feet in a tub of leeches, looking at me with a mixture of pathos and hope.

Like so many of the people in Goldin's photographs from the eighties, my mother also never got the memo that life can swerve from impossible promise to unbearable despair. As a teenager, she had been a shotput champion in college in Jodhpur. In her fifties, she told me that she often waited for the night to end because she had been aching – 'just aching all night' – to move her left leg, but only in the morning hours she might ask someone to help. I kept googling creative, natural ways to cure her bed sores. *Hospital* was a scareword in the lexicon of my childhood. I did not enjoy reading thrillers; I never went to an amusement park because wild rides were not something I'd enjoy. An adrenaline pause, in my life, was a gift. You had to measure your hours between hospital visits, painful for the patient, but distinctively terrible for someone who has to watch a loved one come apart. Decomposition is how organic substances break down into simpler organic matter. This is also called rotting away.

Sometimes, in the afternoons, she wept.

In Laura Esquivel's novel *Like Water for Chocolate* one key character, Tita, weeps from the womb, but the author explains, 'Tita didn't distinguish between tears of laughter and tears of sorrow. For her laughter was a form of crying.' In her essay 'Man, Weeping', the writer Sandra Newman points out that 'weeping was such a central part of worship that it was written into the rules of monastic orders as a required accompaniment of prayer and repentance.' She relates that *The Confessions of St. Augustine* extol the saint's 'unrestrained weeping' while St. Jerome's letter to Eustochium has 'eight separate references to crying'. When the Egyptian goddess Isis finds her brother Osiris dead she weeps over him, and her tears bring him back to life. The confluence of tears and revival in this myth made me wonder about the origins of my mother's own private crying. Was she crying from physical pain, her unending, roiling thing? Or was she trying to bring to life a portion of her life that might never come alive? In *Crying: A Natural and Cultural History of Tears*, Tom Lutz records the 'ritual of laughing and weeping in ancient pre-Hebrew Canaan, traces of which show up in the Hebrew Bible and a number of other sources'. As a springtime ritual, a whole tribe would repair to the desert and commence crying in muffled sobs that escalated to wailing before their collected hysterics dissolved into laughter and giggles that were a preface – or a doorway – back into routine life. 'In these rituals, frantic crying and raucous laughter are not opposed emotional displays but part of a continuum, a continuum based on a belief in emotional expression as a source of fundamental pleasure and social cohesion,' writes Lutz. Yes, that was it, crying foreshadows laughter, they are cyclical, repetitive, indissoluble, perhaps even the same thing.

When I think of what brought my mother any respite, it was always a shard of accidental laughter.

——

'**G**ET me a big, strong vibrator when you come home in the winter,' my mother had called me to say. I was twenty-two, living in the downtown purgatory of San Jose, northern California, a bedsit in a yellow cottage rented out to a pack of student reptiles. My jaw clenched. Was my mother asking me to bring her a personal pleasure device? When I mentioned this to my sister, she clarified: 'She's been watching those horrible home shopping networks; the portable *massagers* are a sellout this season. But they call them vibrators on the telly.' I found a big red vibrator – or massager – at the Kmart in San Jose, where it was stocked next to the bread section. When I gave her the massager that I had bought for her, my mother held it in her arms as if it was a baby.

'I'm going to use my vibrator every day,' she promised me, her eyes welling up.

'I think you can call it a massager.'

She appeared not to heed my suggestion. 'I love my present!'

In my twenties, after the success of my first book, I sometimes hosted dinner parties, which at the time I considered a legitimate form of civic merriment. I felt the particular pride of adhering to ritual: a semi-functional adult male embarking on the bourgeois preamble to a lifetime of phony banter. At one such dinner, as I was serving the food, a scream interrupted the elegant, pointless chatter about the semi-colon's new designation as an affectation.

'Where is my vibrator!'

Guests at the dinner table froze. A few seconds later, my

mother screamed again. 'Where is my vibrator!'

To this dumbstruck gathering of low life-expectancy editors, stilettoed heiresses and frotteuristic diplomats, I explained that my mother was unwell and that she used a massager to relieve her aching muscles. Someone must have moved the massager from its place on her bed, resulting in this impassioned, shrill query. Later, I realized my mother had only been warning me – dinner parties are for deadbeats.

Eleven years have gone by since that dinner and that scandalous scream.

Now, I will never hear my mother's voice.

–

At my bedsit on 12th Street in downtown San Jose, I'd often come back to a voicemail from my mother. But one of them made me feel like I had won the lottery. She had sung my favourite lullaby – *Tamey mara dev na didhail cho*. Her breathing was strained but the tune familiar, a voice like warm soup. The lullaby was like an old white plate with a gold rim, chipped, perfect, handed down with love. More than a song, it was as if she had been praying, a cry to the heavens, a personal azaan.

I had just come home after attending a class on media ethics. On the way, I had stopped to buy a bag of groceries that I had picked up from the local 7-Eleven. As I heard my mother's singing voice, the grocery bags fell out of my hands and I fell to my knees. In *Atonement*, Ian McEwan writes the simplest lines: *I love you. I believe in you completely. You are my dearest one. My reason for life.* Her singing conveyed this to me.

A grown man sobbing is never a pretty sight. Why did the lullaby touch me so deeply? I promised myself I would save that voicemail. A few months later, my phone went bust and I lost my auditory heirloom, a piece of her soul strained to song. When Esquivel's protagonist in *Like Water for Chocolate*, Tita, cries from the womb the tears run down the mother's cheeks.

For me it might be the reverse.

From up above, some of my mother's tears run down my face.

—

The final lesson my mother taught me, and which I also brought to my fiction, was learned in the hospital. When the lights go out in the waiting room of an ICU, around 10 p.m., you get a sense of the afterlife: huddled forms enveloped by the furious whirring of mosquitoes, flatulence released like expletives in a foreign language, a brass band of snorers, jittering arms thrown out in mid-sleep, saliva dribbling from lips. But these people are not dead, even if they do summon the afterlife, or some milder, low-cal version of hell. This hell has a soundtrack. It's a bit of an opera but the music isn't quite what you might expect. A nurse shouts out the name of one patient and the daughter rises from this mass, covers her head in a white dupatta and begins to weep as she walks toward the cold white lights, shedding her shoes, donning white slippers, pumping hand sanitizer for the last time. In the morning, people have the weather-beaten look of refugees – exiled from old, familiar lives, escaping something that they will never truly leave behind. People carry books, magazines, thermos flasks, prayer beads, crosswords. Those who come here often enough, as my sisters and I had for two decades, become graduates in the art of the waiting room, geniuses at unhealthy coping mechanisms. We are able to sympathize with villains in films. The landscape that lies beyond compassion is stoicism. A sudden howling at 4.00 a.m. does not really alarm us; we see it as a general annoyance, and if we had it in us – some final reserve of strength – we might have slapped the suffering man out of it. The ICU in most Indian hospitals is where despair meets expenses, suffering is defeated by death, generalized maiming accompanies the healing of a fractured ankle. Humanity here is in such a narrow, dark corner that you begin to get a taste of all the wars that you have not lived through, the raping, the pillaging, the gassing – all this suddenly makes sense. The pathos of an ICU waiting room might also turn you unbearably compassionate, although this will run dry when you see a grown man playing video games on the chair next to you as his old mother is being intubated a few metres away. Not all creative writing schools come with a degree.

All the numerous privileges of my life – my education, my house, my health – stood cancelled, or rather they were laid bare. Standing before realities both alien and tormented, I could sympathize with everyone: murderers, vandals, men who break up on text, women who abandon their children, people who don't spell the full form of OK (and use 'K' instead). I say I understood them because in the ICU waiting room everyone was only mass and form. Intelligence, morality, beauty were merely variables, reliant on degrees of dispensation. Even good conduct was a consequence of dispensation – to know better, to be allowed to know better. No one, and nothing, could be above your sympathy, although everyone can slide under your exhaustion – it's ok, you're broken, I'm broken, chin up old goat. You can cry for anyone – for the little boy in white pajamas, sitting next to you, asking for his mother. You solve crossword puzzles with people you might otherwise never speak to – old men with faecal matter in their hair.

The ICU is not the Met Ball. It is a Demolition Ball.

You get that quickly.

Your heart soon makes room for everyone, even the vile people who think climate change is just a bad monsoon, for the women who fly on private jets to the Maldives and post selfies from boats, for the jerks who dump dogs outside a pound in north Goa: they emerged from the same faulty mass of no-warranty, no-exchange human clay. I no longer think of anyone as a 'terrible human being' although I might judge them if they don't know it's bad manners to not keep your phone on silent at 2 a.m. in a room full of people who are huddled together while someone nearby is wheezing as she is going out of business. You re-read *Dracula* in cold light and you come to think of it as a sad story of some lonely chap with an eating disorder. Or a Reddit string on 'how to cook a baby rabbit' is only this: cooking and eating, someone has to die.

At the ICU waiting room you internally repeat the words again – Intensive. Care. Unit. *Caring intensively*. The woman in a blue bucket seat next to you begins to speak and you freeze. Someone is going to ask you for a newspaper or a phone charger, best to meet such requests with a closed-doors expression. But you relent, it comes from caring intensively, a story unfolds.

One night, a woman beside me told me an extraordinary thing. She had gone to prison for setting her husband on fire, after years of enduring his violent beatings. The lawyer who had fought her case was struggling for his life with liver cirrhosis. So she came each night with her faded copy of the *Hanuman Chalisa* to pray for him until he died a month later – a death I learned of only because my mother had to return once more to the hospital then, on account of her septicemia. 'I'm now doing tailoring jobs,' the woman told me. 'In case you want to have shirts made.' I asked her if she had learned tailoring in prison. She nodded and told me, 'In prison, sometimes, they throw boiling water on scuffling inmates – that always works.' I made a note of it.

To prevent the king's death, a substitute king or a 'šar pūhi' is elected – a surrogate king, who will die in lieu of the real king, during this astrological upheaval.

I must now tell you one thing: there is no *šar pūhi* – the business of dying is done entirely alone. A close friend had attended a wedding in Italy, where a guest had read aloud the lines of Forster: 'Only connect! That was the whole of her sermon. Only connect the prose and the passion, and both will be exalted, and human love will be seen at its height. Live in fragments no longer.' For me, these words from *Howards End*, so patently fitting for a wedding, had a different resonance. Even as she was dying, my mother was making a writer out of me by teaching me how to listen. I never got any shirts made, though.

Live in fragments no more.

My view of the world would never be that of an intellectual, who relies on the refinement of perception, but of a monk, who believes in prayer, forgiveness, acceptance of all as one. *Only connect*. This was the waiting room, messy and claustrophobic, a cross-stitch of panic and fatigue, the slum of all existence – everything was here, small, terrified, bare, like a rat left out in the rain.

This was my literary education; it was a way of seeing.

Pray for villains. Sometimes you have to eat little rabbits. Listen, listen, listen.

——

As Saraswathi Devi and I raced up the stairs of Nanavati Hospital to reach my mother on 22 January 2008, it was a familiar drill, showing guest passes to the security, rushing past patients on stretchers, avoiding the glances of hangdog-faced visitors. I had come to hate this hospital, this dreadful, deathly place. On this stay, I remember a resident doctor attending to my mother – he looked at her as if she was already gone. He paid no attention even as she screamed and screamed when a nurse tried to insert a central line in her spine, after the veins on her wrists could tolerate no further insertions. I was ready to slap the nurse when she told my mother, 'It's going to hurt a little bit more.'

I looked my mother in the eye and promised her I was going to lead her out of this. She had lost the ability to speak coherently by then but her eyes were flashing with one request – *Put me out of this*. She had brought me into life; now, she was asking me to extinguish her own. Early on during this final stint at the hospital we had asked for her to be administered morphine. But the doctors did not oblige even when she was shouting out in agony. When her health declined further they agreed to a morphine compound which kept her in a deep sleep, bordering the unconscious, for most of the day. This is how she was on that last night – in blackout sleep.

Into a small, private chamber in the ICU my sisters and I gathered at my mother's bedside one last time. The first time Saraswathi met Padmini they burst into tears; later, she said she had felt a connection that transcended this birth. In a letter, years later, she said of Padmini – *I loved her so much*. I felt this then, even as we gathered around my mother, and Saraswathi took us through Padmini's death as a process where we were participant and witness, where we might be lifted out of the horror of her death by an awareness of its strength.

Because she was trained in home deaths, Saraswathi Devi – tall, erect, silver hair streaming down the length of her back – led us through its remarkable theatre.

'Yes,' she told my sister Nehal, 'you can sing to her. Sing into her ears. She doesn't have much time.'

And now my sister sang.

'You can press her feet,' she told Parul, who was weeping. 'She can feel your touch.'

So now my sister rubbed her feet.

'You can tell her how much you love her,' she told me.

I whispered this, over and over again. *Love. Love. Love.*

'I sense beings in the room.' Saraswathi closed her eyes. In such leave-takings she can experience the presence of a group of entities representing the spirit beings – devas, angels. As death advances, these beings, and one's ancestors, envelope the dying in a deafeningly silent expression of love and protection. Sometimes, during passage rites, Saraswathi has seen colours, or light; she has heard internal instructions for who should be there, and what might happen next. 'It can be achingly long,' she had said to me. 'It is always excruciatingly beautiful.'

She said that my mother's ancestors were in the room, waiting and sheltering her. 'It's never in an instant,' she said, 'the break is gradual. The soul slips out, then slips back in – afraid, nervous, unsure.' She alluded to a gentle call from the other side, from the ones who have passed before her. 'I think it is going to be now,' she counseled. When she extended her arms out into the air, she appeared to embrace all the things hidden from us, a tremendous wisdom of time, the beauty of unencountered places. 'See – there it is, the thing is done, now she is free.' Just like that the machines stopped bleeping, the room fell silent, the air grew cold. My sisters and I looked at each other, dazzled, moved, mindful, lifted, as if we had just emerged from the theatre, or the opera, or from listening to a song that, oddly enough, felt like a lullaby.

Even in her death, our mother had been singing to us.

——

A spit of beach in Morjim, where the Chapora river enters the Arabian Sea, is concealed by a grove of pine trees. Ignored by most tourists, its isolation makes it a favourite of middle-aged Russian nudists who live in Goa six months of the year. In the distance is the fort with damaged turrets and embrasures; at its base, another beach with a temple, a quay for fishermen's boats. Birdlife includes plovers, Brahminy starlings, kites. A few years ago, an eleven-foot mugger crocodile accidentally ended up here. A local had shot it on his phone while it was doing its threatening high walk after the neighbourhood dogs began to bother it. On most days I come here to swim in the estuary, where I sometimes see dolphins in the headwaters. I walk the length of the remote beach. Standing against the wind, looking out at sea, the sky is icy blue, without any clouds. At the age of forty-two, I have set aside much of my past, not through erasure but by acceptance. When I am swimming in the sea – as I do each evening – it is possible to go out so deep that you can no longer see the shore. I might feel marooned, helpless, or I might thrill from an overwhelming sense of abandon. A plover comes into view; then, a grove of pines. The shore is there, of course, I can see it: smooth, white sand, undulations. I swim back to this shore, wondering where my mother is. *After all these years, I am still looking for my mother.*

—

Robert MacFarlane wrote a remarkable poem about the lark;
it is also a poem that makes a secret nod to mental health and
depression.

Right now, I need you, for my sadness has come again
And my heart grows flatter – so I'm coming to find
You by following your song
Keeping on into deep space, past dying stars and
Exploding suns, to where at last, little astronaut
You sing your heart out at all dark matter.

——

A FEW years before she died, on the evening of the book launch of *Bhatkan*, my mother's first and only book of poetry, all her friends were by her side: Anila Aunty and Mira Ben, Hansa Ben and Sonal Ben. There was singing, there was laughter, there was a formidable array of snacks. Wheeled out on her bed, my mother lay in the centre of the living room, a deposed queen, but still a queen. Her friends wore red saris and yellow ones; they carried silk clutches and roomy handbags with pill cases and hair clips. They had been part of her satsang group, a set of bright, spirited women who met once a week to discuss sections of the *Bhagavad Gita*. The spiritual nourishment of the *Gita* saw each one of these women through their lives, parenting their anxieties, tempering their grief, extending prayers of hope, relief and splendour. As always, Padmini was consumed with instructing her children to attend to the guests, to refill someone's glass of nimbu sherbet or to bring out a chair. The air was warm and still; from the areca palms in the garden outside, mynahs called out. The sky was brilliantly blue. The kadam trees my father had planted were blooming, as if rejoicing in the event, and their arresting, fragrant scent was like what I had encountered before only in the inner sanctum of a temple.

I had never seen her happier, and now the roles were reversed, she was the published writer and I was her cheering audience. She lay sideways on the bed, I touched her arm, she looked up at me. Catching the eye of her beloved, kind sister, Kumudini, she smiled at her. Kumudini, along with her husband Kiran, had seen my mother through some of the worst years of her life. She would simply ring Kumudini, and no matter what she was doing, she would drop it and take a train out to see Padmini, at home, or in the hospital. Kumudini's acts of kindness are too large and profound for measure. Then she called to her side Urvashi, her – and now my – closest friend. She reminded Urvashi of the many visitors who she had brought to her bedside and for whom she had performed her poems. Urvashi was the only friend who never rolled her eyes at my mother's many absurd dietary claims: eating ghee was beneficial as it lubricated the joints, or that it was best to have one small meal every two hours instead of four fixed ones. But Urvashi never laughed at my mother's 'twelve-meals-a-day' diet. Instead, like an excellent friend, she simply packed Russian salad sandwiches (from the original Tarla Dalal recipe) and brought them to Padmini along with a paan from Mishra Paan Centre, as one of her twelve daily meals. They would relish this together in the afternoon, it was something of a cemetery picnic, Urvashi's sweet, refulgent laughter echoing out of my mother's room like something made from pure silk.

Now, though, Padmini was giddy with happiness, her smile was radiant, her cheeks glowed. So here she was, finally a published poet, a few short years before her death. All her friends were here, her husband and her children too, it was so wonderful, it was just perfect, you could not ask for more, her heart was full, it was overflowing. She began to read 'Bhatkan', her favourite poem from the collection.

———

भटकन

ये शिकवे, ये गिले किसलिए?
ये आरजू ये मिन्नतें किसके लिये?

जीयें तो कुछ ऐसे कि तन्हां न रहें हम
जिनसे हैं, जिनके हैं, उन्हीं से जा मिलें हम।

जिस मंज़िल से चले थे भटकने को,
आ मिले उसी की चौखट पर जब,
राह कुछ सूनी सी रुखी सी न रहे
क्यों न भर दें उसे संतुष्टि-रस से।

जब कभी आ मिलें यकायक मंजिल से
तो पायें और देखें कि वहीं जा पहुँचे हैं, कि
जहां से चले थे उधर ही पहुँचे हैं!
भटक भटक कर फिर वहीं आ पहुँचे हैं!

तभी तो ये सोच और है ये मनन,
कि ये शिकवे ये गिले हैं किसलिए?

क्यों कि जो है,वही तो है जिसे जानना
जो था सदैव से, उसी को पहचानना
फिर ये गिले ये शिकवे किसलिए?
हाँ, ये आरजू ये मिन्नतें हैं,
तुम्हारे ही लिए!

Acknowledgements

Thank you: Abhishek, Alan, Amit Uncle, Ananth, Atul, Bina, Bonita, Bron, Dia, Farrokh, Gran Tan, Hemali, Ishan, Jaya, Lisa, Lou, Lucie, Mark, Mita, Pompe, Saraswathi Devi, Shekhar, Siddhartha, Stina, Sooni, Udayan, Urvashi, Vasudha.

Parts of *Loss* were written at two arts residencies:
India-Europe Foundation for New Dialogues, Italy. Special thanks: Jacques Cloarec, Honorary President, and Sylvain Dumont, Administrator.

One World Foundation, Sri Lanka. Thank you: Kathrin Messner.

Royalties from book sales will benefit an animal shelter in Goa: www.wagoa.com. Do consider adopting before you buy a pet.

To invite the author to read to you and your friends from *Loss* over a virtual platform, please email sdshanghvi@gmail.com.

ABOUT THE BOOK

What does it mean to lose someone? To answer this timeless question, bestselling author Siddharth Dhanvant Shanghvi draws on a string of devastating personal losses – of his mother, of his father and of a beloved pet – to craft a moving memoir of death and grief.

With surgical detachment and subtle feeling, Shanghvi charts the landscape of bereavement as he takes the reader down the dark, winding path to healing. Clear-eyed and intimate, *Loss* is the first work of non-fiction by one of India's most beloved writers of life experience.

ABOUT THE AUTHOR

SIDDHARTH DHANVANT SHANGHVI'S first novel, *The Last Song of Dusk*, won the Betty Trask Award, the Premio Grinzane Cavour, and was nominated for the IMPAC Prize. His second book, *The Lost Flamingoes of Bombay*, was shortlisted for the Man Asian Prize. His most recent book is *The Rabbit & the Squirrel* (with illustrations by Stina Wirsen). A past contributor to *TIME*, the *New York Times*, *Vogue* and other publications, he lives in north Goa.